THE SCARLET S: SUICIDE

What do you do when every day is a struggle and the voices in your head tell you there is a simple way out?

Using God's Word to understand and overcome the suicidal thoughts we've been secretly wearing around like a silent badge of shame...

Melissa White

The Scarlet S: Suicide

Copyright © 2019 Melissa White.
Printed in the United States of America.
First Edition, 2020.
ISBN: 978-1-946467-06-5 (Paperback)
ISBN: 978-1-946467-07-2 (Ebook)
Library of Congress Control Number: 2020906556

All rights reserved. No part of this publication may be reproduced, distributed, or transmitted in any form or by any means, including photocopying, recording, or other electronic or mechanical methods, without the prior written permission of the publisher. For permission requests, email the publisher at UNeedHim2@gmail.com.

National Suicide Prevention Lifeline Call 1-800-273-TALK (8255). Available 24 hours a day.
Crisis Text Line available around the clock by texting HOME to 741741.
General Prayer Ministers available at 1-817-852-6000 or submit a prayer request at www.kcm.org/prayer. They pray the Word in faith with you for any situation.

Amplified Bible, Classic Edition ^{AMPC}
Scriptures taken from the Amplified Bible. Copyright © 1954, 1958, 1962, 1964, 1965, 1987 by The Lockman Foundation. Used by permission.

Amplified Bible 2015 ^{AMP}
Scriptures taken from the Amplified Bible. Copyright © 1954, 1958, 1962, 1964, 1965, 1987 by The Lockman Foundation. Used by permission.

King James Bible ^{KJV}
Scriptures taken from the King James Version (KJV): KING JAMES VERSION, public domain. Scriptures not noted as other translations can be assumed to be KJV or commonly rendered by most translations.

New King James Version ^{NKJV}
Scriptures taken from the New King James Version®. Copyright © 1982 by Thomas Nelson. Used by permission. All rights reserved.

New American Standard Bible ^{NAS}
Scriptures taken from the New American Standard Bible®. Copyright © 1960, 1962, 1963, 1968, 1971, 1972, 1973, 1975, 1977, 1995 by The Lockman Foundation. Used by permission.

New International Version ᴺᴵⱽ
Scriptures taken from the Holy Bible, New International Version®, NIV®. Copyright © 1973, 1978, 1984, 2011 by Biblica, Inc.™ Used by permission of Zondervan. All rights reserved worldwide. www.zondervan.com The "NIV" and "New International Version" are trademarks registered in the United States Patent and Trademark Office by Biblica, Inc.™

New Living Translation ᴺᴸᵀ
Scriptures taken from the Holy Bible, New Living Translation. Copyright © 1996, 2004, 2007 by Tyndale House Foundation. Used by permission of Tyndale House Publishers, Inc., Carol Stream, Illinois 60188. All rights reserved. Used by permission.

The Message Bible ᴹˢᴳ
Scriptures taken from The Message: The Bible in Contemporary English. Copyright © 1993, 1994, 1995, 1996, 2000, 2001, 2002. Used by permission of NavPress Publishing Group.

The Passion Translation ᵀᴾᵀ
Scripture quotations from The Passion Translation®. Copyright © 2017, 2018 by Passion & Fire Ministries, Inc. Used by permission. All rights reserved. ThePassionTranslation.com.

Good News Translation ᴳᴺᵀ
Scriptures taken from the Good News Translation - Second Edition. Copyright © 1992 by American Bible Society. Used by permission.

Berean Study Bible ᴮˢᴮ
The Holy Bible, Berean Study Bible, BSB. Copyright © 2016, 2018 by Bible Hub. Used by permission. All rights reserved worldwide.

…for you ♥…

Contents

Section 1: Triggers 3

- Childhood 5
- Tragedy 10
- Self-Perception/Body Image 13
- Rejection in Relationships or Friendships 17
- Family Struggles 19
- Work/Professional Struggles 22
- Sin (promiscuity) 25
- Being Overwhelmed and Out of Balance (physically or mentally) .. 27

Section 2: Ways to Battle and Overcome 31

- Number One: Jesus! 33
- A Glimpse of My Experiences 36
- Satan is Our Enemy 40
- Internalize God's Word—His Image of You 44
- A Word(s) for Every Struggle 49
- Use Your Sword of the Spirit and Your Spiritual Armor 51
  - Belt of Truth 53
  - Breastplate of Righteousness 55
  - Feet Shod with the Preparation of the Gospel of Peace 58
  - Shield of Faith 61
  - Helmet of Salvation 65
  - Sword of the Spirit 71
- Make Covenant With Others Who Can Intercede For and With You 79
- Make Changes Based on Your Heart's Leading 83
- Forgive 88
- Give God's Word Opportunity in the Every Day 93

Give Yourself Away to Get Out of Yourself 95

Fasting 97

Tithing 100

What if It Seems Like It's Not Working? 105

Appendix: Scripture Arsenal/Lies Exposed 115

My earliest memories of struggling with death were of evil forebodings in adolescence. From the age of twelve or thirteen, I always felt I would die young, like a black cloud over my head. It reminds me of Pig Pen, Charlie Brown's friend in the *Peanuts* comic strip.

A well-respected minister I frequently listen to defines evil forebodings as *an oppressive atmosphere where everything seems gloomy—as if something bad is going to happen, often with no basis of reality or obvious explanation—just a vague, dreaded sense of something evil or wrong*. The ^{AMP} mentions them in Proverbs 15:15 when it says *all the days of the afflicted are made evil by anxious thoughts and forebodings*.

When I was nineteen, those anxious thoughts and forebodings turned to thoughts of not wanting to live. I remember sitting on the edge of my bed with a gun in my hand, hysterically crying to my parents that I just wanted to die. I hadn't actually made any connection or plan that I would do anything to myself with the gun. In fact, the reason I had it was to provide a sense of protection.

You see, I had recently been attacked by a complete stranger, with many of the things you can suppose would happen in that scenario happening. During the eleven minutes it lasted, I was sure I would not escape alive, but I wanted to live….and wanted to die so the attack would be over.

It began a pattern of contemplating life and death, just as Shakespeare did in *Hamlet*, to be or not to be? (Tongue in cheek, that was the question.) Just as Job did when he was enduring a season of severe suffering (Job 6:8-11). Just as Elijah did after encountering Jezebel's priests (1 Kings 19:4). Just as Jonah and Jeremiah did when they were frustrated in their work (Jonah 4:3, 8, Jeremiah 20:14-18).

Just as Paul seemed to do when he said *to live is Christ and to die is gain*. He was mulling over whether it was better *to remain* in this natural realm *in fruitful service for Christ*, or *to depart and be free of this world to the Saviour* he longed to spend eternity with (Philippians 1:21-24).

Every translation bears out that he felt he had a choice in the matter, whether he was facing eminent death by the hand of his accusers—the ones who were imprisoning him—or whether he was just self-reflecting is up to interpretation.

Perhaps you've had thoughts of whether to continue your life. Or perhaps you know someone who is struggling with suicidal thoughts. In sharing my experiences with you, my prayer and hope is that Christ is able to **empower** you to overcome.

It's a very real issue for many of us, and it's long past time that we begin to discuss it, to expose it, to teach how to battle it, and to live **on purpose** in the face of it. That face is the hidden, disguised face of satan himself. Scripture makes it very plain that he has always been *the thief who comes to steal, kill, and destroy* (John 10:10).

(I know that grammatically satan should be capitalized, but I refuse to give him that much honor. He is a small, worthless being and as such, gets only lowercase from me. It's not a typo—it's very intentional.)

Let me share with you some of the triggers that have caused me to have episodes of battling for my very survival. And let me reassure you that whether the battle lasted minutes, hours, days, weeks, months, or years (in the big picture), God was and continues to be faithful to help me overcome **every single time**, every single day, and He **promises** to be faithful to you also!

Section 1: Triggers

Childhood

Oh my, my childhood was sprinkled with misfortune! I was the first child born to my parents, my mom being a fourteen-year-old child herself, and my dad being married to another woman when they first met. He left her to wed my mother when she became pregnant. He was seven years her senior and in the service at the time. My mother and I were living with her parents. On the Fourth of July the year I was born, she and I had gone to visit my father in Fort Knox, when my maternal grandfather murdered my grandmother by tying her up and stabbing her over forty times in the bathroom of our home. He was enraged because she was planning to divorce him. I was less than three months old. This was the pretext of my humble beginnings.

My dad always called me his Boo-Boo, which he meant in an affectionate way from some cartoon he liked; it's his favorite nickname for me, and he only uses it in very special times (birthday cards, etc.). But in my heart, satan whispered for years, countless times, the lie that he called me that because I was his mistake. A mistake. The devil told me repeatedly that I wasn't planned, and I shouldn't have been born. That I changed the course of my parents' lives, and they would have been better off without me.

He's even made me wonder if I was the last straw, the tipping point into tragedy for my grandparents—if the stress of an unwanted teenage pregnancy within the household was part of what drove my grandfather over the edge.

I have a sister two years and a brother three years my juniors. Over the next several years, things were tumultuous, and we were very transient. My parents would separate, reunite, argue, fuss, fight, and eventually remarry other people. During a portion of that time, my father, uncle, and some of their 'associates' became drug-central for our small town. This was before the hard-core drugs society is currently struggling to combat, but I remember seeing our dining table completely covered with bags of marijuana and other types of pills (uppers, downers, Speed,

Quaaludes), and we had a steady stream of strangers coming and going as they made their purchases.

Because it was not uncommon to have unknown visitors, I almost let a man I'd never seen before into our home one day. He came walking up our sidewalk, knocked on our door, and asked to see my mother. I told him she wasn't home at the time, but he could come inside to wait for her. As I started to open the door for him, my uncle (her brother), who had been on the phone in a heated conversation with someone, suddenly shoved me out of the way and confronted the man at the door. It was their father—my grandfather—who had just moments before been released after serving his seven-year prison sentence for murdering my grandmother. The phone call had been from someone at the prison making my uncle aware of his release. I had heard him saying, "Here he comes now," as the man came up the sidewalk, but had no idea who **he** was until their confrontation. This was when I learned that my grandfather had sent my mother a letter to tell her that she was next if she didn't help him after his release. Of course, this led to weeks of nightmares!

When I was in second grade, my mother eloped with a friend of my father's. Upon this revelation, my father shot himself with a hunting rifle. He barely missed his heart and lost a large portion of one of his lungs. We were told it was an accident—the gun had accidentally discharged while he was cleaning it. Sometime later, I came to realize the truth of the situation, and he has continued to struggle with his own episodes of depression and suicidal thoughts sporadically through the years. It's not something we have ever been able to discuss.

Their marriages didn't last, but this inconsistency set a pattern of instability for my siblings and me of constantly relocating, people in and out of our lives, parties, drugs, my father's arrests, various babysitters, and elementary schools all across the city, until I was twelve years old, and we went to live with my paternal grandmother and her husband,

Papaw, in a farmhouse on a couple of hundred scraggly acres in the middle of nowhere.

At my grandmother's house, we lived in poverty. We were very isolated out on the farm and, for quite some time, we didn't even have running water and used an outhouse for a restroom. We wore clothes and shoes that were donated or bought at the Dollar General Store. We ate groundhog, squirrel, turtle, and other animals that could be hunted or found as fresh roadkill, or things she could freeze in stockpile from the grocery. If the local market had chicken on sale for $0.39 per pound, limit two, she would bring ten up to the register and tell them they could check her out in one trip, or she would return five times to purchase them. We grew our own vegetables. We bathed in a cattle trough or in the creek. We hung our laundry on the clothes' line summer and winter. It was an extremely simple and embarrassing life when all of my friends had all of the current comforts—running water, air conditioning, better automobiles, etc.

My grandmother had grown up during the Depression and was a mix of that and her own tumultuous youth and adulthood. She'd run away at the age of thirteen to join the traveling carnival and had married a man within it. He was later killed in a carnival-related accident, and she'd married my grandfather, who was a plumber. They had six children and had just completed building a new brick home when he died from complications shortly after surgery to remove a brain tumor. My father was eleven at the time. My grandmother had to move from that new home, and she continued to have her own set of struggles in the years that followed. She lost one child and home to fire and lost another one of her children to an auto accident. Life had made her hard, and she was much stricter than the times required. We weren't allowed to date, wear make-up, shave (until I was way up in high school and she finally relented—imagine being the girl in the middle- and high-school PE locker rooms who couldn't shave in a culture and time when shaving was the norm), get our driver's licenses or anything other children our age were doing.

When we were punished, we would pick our own switch that was used on our legs, have our bare bottoms whipped with a belt, or one of her frequent choices was to use the blade of her twelve-inch butcher knife. She would hold our fingers bent back and down at a ninety-degree angle and use that knife to spank our palms or use a yardstick in the same way.

One day, in a heated argument about what my friends were allowed to do, I told her that I hated her. She smacked me so suddenly and so forcefully across the cheek of my face, it felt my head would spin completely around. I never said anything that disrespectful to her again! I am grateful to her for taking us in and keeping us together (my siblings and me) when we had nowhere else to go, and we had special times together, but overall, she felt more like a grandmommy dearest than someone I could enjoy being around.

And then there was Papaw. A convict my grandmother had married after my grandfather had died. He was a dirty old man, to say the least, and a pervert to be exact. He was a cursing alcoholic denied his alcohol by my grandmother's threats. When we were small, he would try to make games out of showing you his crab pinchers in your privates and asking you to feel the mouse in his pocket until my grandmother found out and threatened to crack his skull wide open with her iron skillet if he ever did it again. As we grew, he would sneak to be the staring face in the window when we were changing clothes. He would stick his tongue in your mouth if you tried to kiss him goodnight on your way to bed, so I quickly learned to skip that gesture and just offer one to my grandmother. He also sat in his chair that no one else ever sat in at the corner of the living room with his body slightly forward at times and his male parts hanging from holes in his pants over the edge of the chair. After a couple of mortifying double-takes when walking through the room, I finally trained myself to not look in his direction when passing. I've never figured out why my grandmother didn't notice or fix the holes in his pants when she did the laundry, and of course, I never mentioned it. Such things weren't approachable conversation.

He passed away unexpectedly early one morning as we were getting ready for school during my junior year of high school. I watched him shaking and gurgling in his throat as he lay on the kitchen floor dying from a heart attack, and in the very core of my being, in the midst of hysterics at watching someone slip into eternity—I feel almost guilty to admit—I also felt relief. I didn't realize what a threat his presence had been to me until the threat was gone.

During a portion of the time we lived at my grandmother's, my uncle moved himself and his family back from another state and lived with us there. Into that dilapidated three-bedroom farmhouse, we crowded thirteen people—three adults and ten children. Laundry and other chores drastically increased, and there were episodes of lice, pinkeye, or some further problem constantly. Collectively, we were like the Herdman's in *The Best Christmas Pageant Ever*.

Maybe your childhood has some incidences within it that made you feel worthless or of little value, insecure, unwanted, or unplanned. Maybe you felt out of control and a casualty to the unpredictable paths it took. Like me, you possibly had your self-esteem marred by things that have happened to you in your formative, developmental years. Or perhaps there has been someone in your family who has struggled with mental illness (my maternal grandfather) or depression (my father) so that there is a chance your struggles have a genetic component to them. This time period in my life set me on very shallow footing for self-worth and confidence.

Tragedy

After being separated for most of my childhood, my parents reunited when I was a senior, and our family was precariously patched back together. They had done a lot of growing up in those years.

As I mentioned before, the tragedy that really started my fierce encounter with suicidal thoughts—the first time I ever remember questioning whether I should live or die—was when I was attacked at the age of nineteen. I had just graduated high school a year before as Salutatorian of my senior class with an impressive 4.12 weighted GPA, an ACT score of 28 (recentered), and a scholarship to Georgetown College, a private Baptist college that was the only place for me! I was the first person in my family to attend college, and I had no idea what I wanted to be (an English major, a journalist, an astronaut, varied and endless possibilities). Although my past was turbulent (a very transient childhood, as stated), my future was bright!

In my first year at Georgetown, I was all but drowned with too much freedom too quickly. I had never really struggled academically in high school or had to spend much effort studying. Good grades pretty much came naturally to me, so I thought I could carry that same nonchalance into my college efforts. The professors at that time only required that you show up for tests. (Most courses now have attendance requirements for a passing grade.)

Boy, did I run in the wrong direction with that! I was at every campus social possible most days of the week. I was experimenting with alcohol for the first time. I was becoming increasingly promiscuous (and breaking the virginity promise I'd made to myself and God), which brings its own set of shameful thoughts no matter how much you declare your new age "I am woman" sexual independence. I ended my first year with a 2.86 GPA and an even more bruised ego.

I had just returned home for the summer a few short days before, when I decided to be out much later than my curfew because my parents were gone overnight with friends. I found myself alone at 2:00 am on a neighborhood street stopping by to see a friend who hadn't been home a few minutes before, so I thought he would still be up to let me in. When he didn't answer because he'd promptly fallen asleep, I was attacked on the way back to my car by someone who was out thieving in the same neighborhood, on the same street, near the same house I was attempting to visit. (When I look back at the youthful foolishness of my past-curfew defiance, it's harrowing.)

The next eleven minutes were hell on earth.

Rape is a crime of anger and rage. I was badly beaten to the point of briefly blacking out, stripped down, raped, sodomized, threatened with death (that each blow of his fist, bash of my head against the ground, and choke-hold around my throat promised to deliver), sickeningly complimented, cursed, and demeaned to my very core. It seemed like an eternity. I still believe he wouldn't have left me there alive if someone hadn't heard me scream and called the authorities who startled him into running as they approached.

I lie there during the course of this, unsuccessfully trying to fight without strength, thinking of my family and how they'd feel knowing what had happened to me, thinking of how I should pray and ask God to help me but falsely thinking within myself that I would be a hypocrite to ask Him for help after the dishonorable year I had spent at college. I was so full of shame. I wanted to live but became convinced I would die.

And then it was over. I was safe again.

But it wasn't really over. I wasn't really safe. In my heart and mind, I relived it repeatedly. I was so full of humiliation. I was mortified of the dark—home or away from home. I slept with a butcher knife under my pillow and carried a gun in my purse. I avoided car garages, elevators, side streets, and anywhere I might meet another individual alone. I was suspicious of everyone. I was living in immense pain and almost constant fear. It was exhausting. This was a preface for suicidal thoughts, wondering if it would have been less painful to have just died during the attack.

Perhaps you've also been through some sort of catastrophe that has deflated you, taken the wind out of your sails, and severely impacted your life. Whether (or not) it was violent, whether it was instigated by a stranger, a friend, a relative, a coworker, or someone else, tragedy has a way of making us question the very foundations of who we are and why we're here.

Self-Perception/Body Image

Something else that has been a recurring struggle for me is my body image and how I feel about myself. I have forever been a hypersensitive person who carries my heart on my sleeve, and I know it has its foundations in my childhood. There has always been **one** thematic voice that has consistently, methodically whispered the same set of lies to my heart through various people and faces from as far back as I can remember. That voice has told me I am ugly and worthless more times than I could possibly count. That it would be better if I'd never been born.

The earliest time I remember hearing it was in first grade when I liked a boy in my class, and one of my friends told him. I thought he was so cute, but his response in learning of my fondness for him was to exclaim in disgust that he thought I was ugly. I was crushed! I cried despairingly! It went straight into my heart like a hardy seed planted in fertile soil, except that it was as robust and harmful as kudzu, an invasive and strangling exotic species.

My heart heard these lies throughout my youth and adulthood through various things that occurred at home and school. My grandmother was one conduit of that voice. She would get frustrated with me and exclaim, "You think you're so pretty, don't you? Pretty is as pretty does!" and "You're so stupid to be so smart!"

The guys at school always called me by my last name like I was one of them (partly because of my strict upbringing that didn't allow us ways to appear more feminine), and this added to my low self-esteem as if they didn't even recognize I was female. Then there was a repeat of my first-grade horror when my ultimate crush from high school—whom I adored as a Greek god, even down to his beautiful feet—told a group of friends at band camp he also thought I was ugly. The traitor who broke my confidence and betrayed my crush to him couldn't wait to let me know what he'd said in response to my affection. It took me forever to recover from that.

By the time I was an adult, I felt so damaged and broken, especially after being attacked, it's no wonder I married someone who was completely wrong for me. Someone with whom the broken pattern would continue. Tumultuous. Unstable. Someone who regularly told me how ugly I was, cursed me, acted insanely jealous, and made statements like, "You could pick corn with your teeth."

I would be singing on the worship team and look out at him in the congregation and he would be making scornful, exaggerated faces like I was this repulsive, sickening person who didn't deserve to be let out in public—like someone who didn't deserve to BE—period.

At home, I remember trying to lock the bathroom and bedroom doors because he would follow me around after my shower telling me how disgusting and ugly I was. On one occasion he lay on the bed watching me trying to quickly get dressed and literally sounded like he was about to vomit (you would have been convinced he was actually getting sick if you hadn't known it was a ploy just to be cruel), and he was saying how disgusted it made him just to look at me.

He would spit on me. He would throw, hit, and break things (phones, remotes, doors, windshields) and drive enraged at eighty miles an hour down neighborhood streets. One day, we were hit when he ran a red light while arguing. Other than putting his hand on my throat on one occasion and threatening to choke me over a purchase he wanted to make, and shoving me around a few times, once into a wall, most of the abuse was mental. But mental scars can be much more permanent than physical scars, and just as painful.

I prayed so much for him and our marriage. I used to send for prayer cloths and put them under his pillow and purchase anointing oil to put on him while he was asleep. I really wanted my commitment to marriage to be something that **worked**. I was grasping for a fairytale he couldn't deliver.

I fasted, prayed, searched the Word, and sought wisdom with all I had within me. In my exasperation, I used to pray that God would just take me—just take me on to Heaven. I couldn't even get a knife out of the drawer to slice something that the voice wouldn't tell me to just go ahead and cut my wrists and put myself out of the misery I was living in. Or drive my car into the next semi I passed or into the river. Or take every pill in the medicine cabinet. It seemed inescapable and never-ending. (I knew the voice was a lie that I shouldn't listen to, but it had become almost constant.)

Then his actions accelerated to include drug use and adultery. We had a small son, five at the time, who was beginning to act like him. He'd get angry and curse me too. After seven years of living like this, I finally felt a release from God to divorce him. At this point, I had incontestable biblical grounds to do it. I ran and didn't look back, although the actual divorce took over four years and so many court battles to accomplish that it is a story within itself.

Along with the damaged roots of my childhood and youth, this had left me with not only low self-esteem, but a body image of being completely unattractive. I would look in the mirror and see this hideous and repulsive person whose teeth were too large and whose nose was huge. It didn't help that I have a birthmark on my back the size of a salad plate and shaped like a state map. I hated myself. I actually walked physically slouched over to a degree because the oppression was so heavy.

I would look at others and see this beauty in them that I longed to have. I remember this lady at church who was wheelchair bound and suffering from many health issues, as well as obesity, and I told God that I wished I could trade places with her because I could see beauty within her I couldn't find within myself.

Sometime after this I was in the kitchen at my parent's house while the television was on *Dr. Phil* or some such show, and I heard someone speaking **my** thoughts out loud. She was talking about how she perceived herself as disgustingly unattractive and she felt that her nose was too big and her smile was unsightly, on and on. I immediately related to her plight like she had looked into my very soul. She was diagnosed with a disorder called Body Dysmorphic Disorder (BDD).

According to Wikipedia, it is defined as *a mental disorder characterized by the obsessive idea that some aspect of one's own body part or appearance is severely flawed and warrants exceptional measures to hide or fix. Often, the flaw is imagined, and if it is actual, its importance is severely exaggerated. Either way, the thoughts about it are pervasive and intrusive and can occupy several hours a day. Its severity can wax and wane, and flare-ups tend to yield absences from school, work, or socializing. It usually starts during adolescence and can be attributed to an interaction of multiple factors, including genetic, developmental, psychological, social and cultural. Many patients note earlier trauma, abuse, neglect, teasing, and/or bullying. It affects both men and women. It can severely impair quality of life and has high rates of suicidal thoughts and suicide attempts.*
(https://en.m.wikipedia.org/wiki/Body_dysmorphic_disorder)

Finally, albeit self-diagnosed, I had a name to put with these redundant feelings and the source of the cause of part of my affliction, culminating from a lifetime of adverse experiences. But knowledge is power and being able to label it helped me to recognize and resist it.

Some or more of this might be relatable to you as a cause of your feelings of low self-worth. Maybe unpleasant and traumatic experiences or abusive relationships have left you emotionally scarred. Perhaps that same criticizing voice has spoken to you through different people and experiences telling you that your life has no value either. But take hope because that voice is not a voice of truth at all and only lies to us. We can be eternally and refreshingly relieved to learn life-changing, timeless Truth about ourselves. We do not have to be victims of those self-defeating lies any longer! Keep reading, friend!

Rejection in Relationships or Friendships

As you can imagine, and as it stands to reason after everything I've described to you, my ability to trust has at times been much diminished. As a newly single mom who didn't want to bring men in and out of my son's life and who was also focused on returning to school to obtain my elementary education degree, I had little time for relationships. I definitely wanted one, but I wanted it to be from God, God-ordained and God-blessed, so maybe this time it would actually work without being so much work, and this time I wouldn't have to struggle to maintain a positive self-esteem and identity.

I seldom dated and usually found rationale to not like the person when I did. I had a wall up for what seemed like good, solid reasons, and it was very rarely that I took my guard down.

But when I did, I jumped in with both feet—rushed in even—willing to love wholeheartedly and give without reservation. The flipside to that—my Achilles heel—is that I am the world's worst at dealing with rejection or giving up. I have this bull-dog tenacity within me that can be unintentionally misdirected but is very helpful when channeled properly. But unfortunately, that same tenacity has blinded me at times from knowing when to call it quits.

The first big relationship I had was four years after my divorce began. I didn't think I liked him at first, but he spoiled me and treated me like I've never been treated before (helping me immeasurably when I was used to doing everything by myself, flowers, cards, gifts, romantic letters, dates, trips, promises of unending love). He was even willing to help me "keep my virginity" this time (the promise I'd made to God when I was a little girl). We became inseparable.

Before I knew it, I was hopelessly head over heels and absolutely adored him. So much so that I didn't see many of the issues he had brought into the relationship, and I had enough of my own too. (I truly believe many times we don't see another person's issues because they put on their best selves at first, not showing us who they really are until later.)

But two years in, after I had loaned over a thousand dollars to him (which to his credit he eventually paid back) and things began to fall apart quickly as if a rug had been pulled out from under my magic happily ever after, I was completely crushed...again. There was little explanation. We weren't even friends afterward, not by my choice, and I began to reel emotionally in the wake of it. I got drunk for the first time in years, and then again and again, for a few weeks. I literally wanted to die. Again. The pain was **so** immense.

I began to pray and fast and try to hold out hope for the relationship, long after I should have used those same spiritual efforts to let God heal me and move on. I've always wanted to "fix" things that were important to me instead of releasing them. (There is an occasion for both depending on the situation, but I realized later this was an occasion to let go.) I missed opportunities with my son and my family during this extended time of mourning when I was present but not really there due to my overwhelming grief.

When I got to the other side of that, I determined never again to let the ending of a relationship have such an effect on me. I will never again mourn a man who has decided for whatever reason I am not the fit for him that he needs. But that strength comes a lot from knowing how much our Lord values me, and that's a conversation for another chapter. That buoyancy is available to us all. If you've faced overwhelming grief at loss or rejection, whether it's the result of a failed relationship or friendship, or perhaps even the death of a loved one, you too can be triumphant over those crippling feelings through Christ!

Family Struggles

Before returning to school, I was able to stay home with my son from the time he was born until he started first grade. Even during my divorce, it worked out that I could be home with him through kindergarten while providing childcare for my sister. I wouldn't trade one minute of those precious years, and we were very close and affectionate. But as I mentioned before, my son had seen (and begun to mimic) the way his father treated me for some of his formative years. Even after the divorce, while I was awarded full custody, he had visitations with him where his father would make me the scapegoat for all of his woes and misfortunes.

As my son grew older, his father basically programmed him to be angry toward me and to have a negative outlook toward women in general. Because of his many troubles with any form of authority in his life, whether a boss or law enforcement, he also taught him to have a disrespect toward authority. This has caused my son many problems throughout his youth and into his young adulthood. He has had to relearn and reprogram the way he thinks, responds, and acts in his everyday life. He now tells me it was his father who gave him such terrible guidance, who told him he shouldn't listen to anyone who tried to tell him what to do, whether it was me, a teacher, or anyone else. He now regrets listening to his advice and realizes it was very reckless and misguided.

But before these revelations, during his middle and high school years, this was a source of constant struggle between us as he would get into trouble at school, fighting, cussing teachers, not turning in assignments, throwing desks across classrooms, just anything to appear rebellious and intimidating. Then he would bring that attitude home and turn it on me when I would support the teachers and demand better from him. He had always been a distinguished student academically before this, and I knew what he was capable of so I would refuse to budge from administering consequences.

He became the voice I had temporarily silenced by divorcing his father. Now he expressed hatred for me on a regular basis. He thought I was stupid, mean, and crazy. "Crazy" was frequently his key word to inflict hurt. I know teenagers often go through this phase with their parents, but he pushed the envelope. He started putting holes in doors and breaking things when he was angry and getting up in my face to curse and intimidate me like he wanted to hurt me. He began experimenting with drugs and running away from home.

My family tried to help. He lived temporarily with my parents and my sister, but after a honeymoon period where they would start to wonder if I had exaggerated, he would soon display similar problems there, and they would deliver him back to me with apologies for their well-intentioned intervention.

I was at my wit's end, and the voice was back, questioning my will to live. When I would try to tell my son how sad it was making me and appeal to his sense of reason, it would always backfire and fuel his "crazy" argument. Then the voice would tell me that if I went through with it, it would prove to him I had been seriously struggling with suicide. It would surely make him sorry! But my tenacity would kick in and not let me give up. I was in a battle for both of us, really.

Through much prayer and seeking direction, I filed a beyond control order on him and had him placed at an alternative living facility, Cumberland Adventure Program, for nine months. God brought people into my path (a concerned professor from my college, a wonderful lady at the facility, an amazing social worker, and a wise judge) at just the right time who helped accomplish this like a much-needed, huge door swinging wide open at just the right time. He finished high school there, reflected upon and regrouped his thoughts and actions, was baptized shortly after coming home, and was able to better discern good influences from bad ones in his life. He was so apologetic and appreciative of the support he finally realized I had always tried to give him. I had made nine months of Sunday trips every week (even on his absent dad's weekends) with all of his favorite home cooked meals in tow, written letters constantly, and called every time he was allowed phone privileges. His dad never visited—not once.

We've still had our ups and downs, and he has gone through many more mistakes he seems to have learned valuable lessons from, but this phase was the one that practically did me in.

Family struggles, especially when your children are involved, are as close to home as it gets. The devil wants to use them as ammunition against us to hurt us, steal our peace, keep us in a state of chaos and confusion, and ultimately destroy us, but God has grace and wisdom for us in every situation to help us overcome. We have to keep our hope because there is a solution to every problem—and suicide is NEVER a valid solution no matter how strong the temptation is.

Work/Professional Struggles

Something else that has triggered very painful feelings for me are struggles I have had in my career. Schools are generally made up of a majority of women. (We desperately need more male teachers and role models!) And women can be some of the most vicious creatures anyone can encounter, even though we were created with such a nurturing, mothering nature.

Women love to gossip and will stab you in the back while smiling to your face. I have had this happen to me on more than one occasion. If someone feels threatened by you or jealous of you for any reason, the rumors start. This can catch you off guard and be especially painful.

I remember my first classroom year, in a collaboration room with twenty-nine students (over the cap limit for teacher/student ratio), several of whom had some serious and life-threatening disabilities and ailments. Two of them could possibly die if someone who had ingested peanuts even breathed on them. One of them had a history of seizures. One of them had intricate heart surgery mid-year. Another one of them had been institutionalized several times, and two others were later considered for referral for behavior disorders. One of them had lost a hand at a very young age and was learning to accommodate questions from his classmates about his perceived difference. I also had several English as Second Language (ESL) students. They all had such varied academic levels and needs and a medley of backgrounds in their home lives. Some had strong, two-parent homes while others were living in single-parent homes or with other relatives. Two of them were coming to school with bed bugs still crawling on them.

It was sink or swim for me as it took everything within me regarding taking them from where they were academically and getting them to where they needed to be. Just a typical, normal day within the classroom was a challenge, but then the tales started.

I was called in to discuss several issues that had twisted or no truth to them. Was my parent volunteer teaching my class? Why did she show up so often? Were my kids not getting recess? Why did I allow them to have lunch in the room with me more than other teachers did? Why was my Facebook so "fanatical"? People were talking about all of the Jesus devotionals I was posting and all of the Scriptures I put on my timeline—it was implied that I appeared like some sort of Jesus freak.

This conversation took place right before spring break, and I literally spent the first three days of break in the bed in full-blown depression fighting suicidal thoughts anew and again while in complete despair.

I had to choose on purpose to walk in forgiveness and take the high road so those offensive feelings didn't continue to derail my faith, my purpose, and my daily life. Since then, there have been other rumors and accusations that were also not fact-based or truthful on even the slightest level.

But satan's attacks are very often not really **new**—just systematic, persistent, and relentless. His goal is to wear us down, but in Christ, we have a constant source of strength, grace, and tenacity within the fruits of the spirit provided by the Holy Spirit (Galatians 5:22-23).

Perhaps in your career or workplace things haven't played out fairly, and you question yourself or your calling because of it. Our occupations often assume an extremely large part of our identity, and it is easy to feel like a complete loser when unjust things happen in relation to them, but this is a natural response for most people because of the high degree of investment we bring into our livelihoods.

And our colleagues with whom we have common purpose often become our "work family" so betrayal by them runs very deep within us. It was Daniel's colleagues who maliciously betrayed him and had him thrown into the lion's den (Daniel 6:1-16), and Jesus Himself was betrayed by one of His own disciples whom He loved very much, someone who should have understood His purpose and heart more than most people would (Luke 22:47-48).

But the good news is that God wants to be our Justifier and Defender, and He promises that *no weapon formed against us shall prosper and every tongue that rises against us shall be shown to be in the wrong* (Isaiah 54:17).

Sin (promiscuity)

I have also brought struggles upon myself due to my own negative choices. Sin will yield feelings that work against our soundness of mind and spirit. That's because large-scale and smaller scale, the wages of sin is death. Of course, we seldom die immediately, though some sins can lead to immediate death (experimenting with drugs can lead to drug overdose, drinking and driving can lead to a fatal accident, etc.), but the spiritual Truth is that if we continue in sin, it works against us—spirit, soul, and body—because it condemns our hearts before God and embarrasses us out of accessing His loving assistance when we need it. This condemnation keeps us from receiving from God and experiencing the fullness of peace and joy Christ has for us in our everyday lives and in overcoming challenges in our path.

Just as I mentioned earlier, my shameful year at college when I was eighteen and nineteen years old kept me from asking God for help in one of the most critical events of my life...I literally could not call out to Him due to the mountain of condemnation that was present in my heart and mind over my promiscuous choices.

This has happened since then in my nineteen-plus years of being single since my divorce. That is a long time to be celibate and without natural affection when we are designed to have intimacy as one of our biological needs and desires. In the times I have strayed from my celibate path, I have faced remorse and shame (in direct confrontation to the righteousness Christ provides me) brought on by the conflict between my carnal and spiritual natures.

Perhaps you also have some type of sin that has caused you to struggle in ways you wouldn't have otherwise had to struggle and brought unnecessary battles into your life. God is faithful to remove our transgressions from us when we come to a place of repentance—true remorse and change that takes the condemnation from our souls and shows us instead His loving conviction that leads to restoration and renewed confidence before Him. And He is powerful enough to deliver us from every temptation, addiction, or bondage when we seek Him (1 Corinthians 10:13). He strongly desires that we be free and blessed. *He came to give us full, abundant, overflowing life* (John 10:10 ᴬᴹᴾ).

Being Overwhelmed and Out of Balance (physically or mentally)

In times when I have experienced extended periods of being overwhelmed with work, school, or home (or a combination of them), it has also been a fight to not want to throw in the towel and quit. These feelings of being engulfed in the everyday can easily cause all of the areas of our lives to feel out of balance and hopeless, especially when it goes on for a lengthy period of time. We may not be able to see light at the end of the tunnel.

For instance, being a teacher necessitates many more hours than some professions involve, and in trying to keep up with the daily requirements it presents, especially with any added periodical deadlines or challenges, I have often found myself staying later than I intended or even leaving school at midnight. With a schedule like this, there is not enough time for proper rest, exercise, healthy food choices, or sustaining the other requirements that make life more manageable. I have often said if home is maintained (clean laundry and dishes, housework caught up), school is a mess, and vice versa. I know many teachers face this struggle, and I'm sure it is not unique to only teaching. Personal health and fitness are always at the top of my desires but the bottom of my to-do list. Before I know it, I've packed on extra weight, I'm wearing the same pair of pants twice before I get a chance to wash them, and life just feels out of control.

This is especially true if any extenuating circumstances are added. Teachers are frequently required to move entire classrooms and switch grade levels during summers. Overcrowded classrooms often have several students who face unfair and heartbreaking struggles we emotionally shoulder with them. Personal circumstances arise within our own families. Health issues become more frequent in extended times of imbalance. Grief from any kind of loss can throw off our balance.

There may even be a medical reason we feel more incapable of handling the everyday requirements of life. For instance, a few years ago I remember just feeling like I did not have the energy to live. I wrote about it in my prayer journal. There was nothing blatantly "wrong" that I could put my finger on. I would make it through the school day, over snack for energy, and then quickly crash when I got home. I felt drained all the time. I felt depressed without an obvious reason.

Eventually symptoms started to compound, and I went to the doctor. I had started having a ringing in my ears, shortness of breath, dizziness upon standing, irregular heartbeat at times, and finally, a crawling sensation all over my midsection that I was worried was scabies (although there were no visible signs). With blood tests, I realized I was extremely anemic and all of these symptoms were a result, even the severe depression I had started to feel. With a few months of extra iron intake, the symptoms started to recede, and I felt some sense of balance coming back.

Sometimes the feelings of imbalance can be from a mental or spiritual source though. More recently, at a late summer request, I had moved my classroom within just two short weeks of school beginning. (I have moved classrooms five times in eight years, and the physical and emotional requirements this brings with it are enormous!) There was so much to accomplish during this time as I had to sift through a large amount of things the prior room occupant had left, as well as move and assimilate my own classroom possessions into this space. I worked long hours (even one continuous thirty-six-hour period at a crunch time) so I was definitely setting myself up for physical exhaustion. I felt like I hit the ground running and didn't have time to breathe. By October, my late nights were back and any of the balance I had previously acquired was in the rearview mirror. Then twice in the same week, I slipped and fell on floors that had recently been mopped. The first time, I thought, oh well, that was silly—you saw her mopping! But I had forgotten by the time I went to leave a short while later.

The second time, later that week, I had no idea the lobby had just been mopped and was rushing out to get home, after 8:00 pm, with a million things on my mind, and unexpectedly found myself on my back, with all the dread, confusion, and surprise that comes from something you didn't expect suddenly happening. It took me a few seconds to figure out what had occurred. I was in pain physically, but much worse than that, my heart was broken—my spirit was crushed. Something inside me just snapped. For the next several months—probably one of the longest continuous times I've experienced it—all the suicidal thoughts were whispering in my ear again. I knew from my past experiences with them how to get through them and not to trust them, but it took me what felt like an eternity to break through and feel like I had gotten to the other side of them. (I'll relate it to trying to navigate through a dark, dreary forest, and then finally breaking through to a clearing.)

Identifying triggers for suicidal feelings is an important step to being able to work through them and overcome them. In understanding what has prompted them, we can take appropriate measures to resist and defeat them. In the next section, we'll look at ways to overcome these debilitating thoughts and tools that empower us to defeat them.

Section 2: Ways to Battle and Overcome

Number One: Jesus!

I know there are many support organizations for anything today's person could possibly encounter, self-help books by the dozens in any area of interest or need, crisis hotlines for any expanse of misfortune, rehabilitation centers, qualified therapists, medications, etc., and I would not even begin to judge or diminish their ability to be of assistance to someone in personal struggles, but I cannot stress enough the OVERWHELMING NEED FOR CHRIST in our daily lives and our imminent eternity. Especially if you have reached the point of considering taking your own life—your most valuable possession—an eternally irreversible decision, what do you have to lose at this point by accepting Him?

You have **nothing** to lose in making a decision to give your life to Him, and a **covenant future** to **gain.** He is a covenant, loving, faithful God in spite of anything otherwise you may have heard or been taught. You might fall anywhere on a spectrum of little to no knowledge of Him to an intellect with many years of religious teaching and experience.

But I implore you as a critical first step in taking control of these debilitating and paralyzing suicidal thoughts to sincerely consider your relationship with Him, be willing to lay aside everything you think you know, and pray this prayer regardless of your previous religious experiences. Acts 2:21 says *whosoever shall call upon the name of the Lord* for help *shall be saved*, and Romans 10:9 says *if you will confess with your mouth Jesus as Lord and believe in your heart that God raised Him from the dead, you will be saved*. Pray this prayer out loud, even if it's a whisper:

> Dear Heavenly Father, Lord Jesus, and Holy Spirit, I need You! I've come to the point in my life where it feels I cannot go on and I'm not sure if I want to, but I'm willing to give it to You—my life—and see what You can do with it and where You can take me. Help me to be obedient to follow Your promptings in my heart, to see Your path clearly through any confusion,

and to be patient and resolute while You work to improve things on my behalf. I call upon You for salvation, and I confess Jesus as my Lord that God raised from the dead. I also ask You to fill me with Your Holy Spirit to be my Guide and Teacher! In Jesus' Name, Amen!

In asking the Holy Spirit to fill you, you have just accepted the best Teacher you could ever have to help you in your efforts to overcome daily challenges and become increasingly successful in every aspect of life! Jesus promised in John 14:16-26 that Father God would send the Spirit *to fill us, be our constant Advocate, remind us of God's Word* in order to apply its Truth to our lives, and *teach us all things*. (Wow! There was no parameter placed on that—He didn't say all spiritual or religious things; He simply said **all** things. That can mean wisdom in any context in our home and work lives! What an exciting and useful promise!)

And the best news of all is that it doesn't matter your past, your age, your race or gender, your physical circumstances, your prior religious experiences (or lack of), or any other distinguishing factor—God will use the decision you just made and the Holy Spirit within you to improve everything. Some changes will seem immediate and some will be more gradual, but you have just entered into a covenant arrangement with the God of the universe, and He takes you very seriously. In fact, He is **wildly in love** with each one of us and wants to be as involved as we'll let Him in even the smallest details of our lives (Psalm 37:23 [NLT]; Romans 8:28 [MSG, TPT], Matthew 10:30 [MSG, TPT], James 5:11 [MSG])!

Jeremiah 31:3-4 [AMP] tells us God *has always loved us with an unfailing, everlasting love, draws us with His lovingkindness*, and wants to be *faithful continually to us*. He wants *to rebuild us* to the point that we have reason to *celebrate*. The [MSG] version says we can *start over*. That's great news if we need a fresh start!

Ephesians 1:4 tells us that *in His love, Jesus chose us before the foundations of the world*. Psalm 139:16 [MSG] says *He formed us in our mother's wombs so that we are marvelously made, body and soul*, and *He knows us* completely, *how we were sculpted from nothing into something. All the days of our lives He has planned and prepared before we even lived one of them.* So, you see, we are not mistakes. We are planned and wanted and deeply loved. We just have to get with His plan!

The steps contained within Section Two that follow will help us do that. They aren't intended as a formula for religious "works" nor are they meant to overwhelm us while we strive to implement them or if (when) we mess any of them up, but they are a solid plan to help us make forward progress and grow in relationship with our loving and faithful God. He won't ask or expect us to rapidly be expert at them as we learn to apply them, but rather to be led by His Spirit within us as we aim to advance past suicidal feelings, anxiety, and depression, and give each day the best we have at the time.

Matthew 6:34 [MSG] tells us to *give our entire attention to what God is doing right now, and not get worked up about what may or may not happen tomorrow because God will help us deal with whatever hard things come up when the time comes.* Philippians 1:6 assures us that Jesus will continue to be patient with us and help us as we strive to make positive growth on a day by day basis. One day at a time. I can handle that, and so can you!

So then, the key to using these steps is to make relationship with Him the focus, the momentum, and the end goal because in this relationship is grace, strength, mercy, favor, and more **love** than we will ever realize this side of Heaven (Ephesians 3:19).

A Glimpse of My Experiences

In my own life, I have had this innate love for Jesus as far back as I can remember. I don't ever think there has been a time I questioned His existence, and for that I am very grateful. Even at five years old, I recall taking the church bus alone to the church in our neighborhood to attend Sunday School classes. When we would visit my grandmother, and later when living there, I always caught rides with friends, relatives, and neighbors to attend nearby country churches. In younger years, I would go alone (as far as members of my family were concerned) and in later years, my sister would often come with me, and occasionally our brother would join us. For years and years, I never missed a service and attended an array of Christian and Baptist locations. (My dad took my siblings and me to visit a Pentecostal church once, and I got the daylights scared out of me between the praying in tongues, people running the perimeter of the sanctuary, and old ladies being 'slain in the spirit' while sitting in their pews! At ten years old, that was a little too strange for me.)

I was diligently searching for God during those years while placing myself repeatedly in the very places I was supposed to be able to find Him. It seemed that although I had my ticket to Heaven, I just had to hang on until I could get there. Most of my knowledge of God was either lack of information or misinformation. We, as members of the congregations I attended, were perpetually dangled over hell to keep us repentant and reassured that when we got THERE (Heaven), life would be glorious.

I attempted to read my Bible several times over those years. After reading the novel *Fahrenheit 451* during one of my high school classes, I even had the noble intention of memorizing it as some of the characters in that story had for the day the books would be burned. I would get a couple of chapters into Genesis and give up because I was taking the "word for word" memorization approach and not the "jest of it", story-based approach. I always had several chapters to report toward our Sunday School tallies, but I couldn't make it past the first few books of the Old Testament since most of my efforts were to begin at the beginning and read through.

After I was attacked at nineteen years old, the person who attacked me was arrested in pretty short order while trying to pawn something he'd stolen that night. I identified him through a photo line-up, and his trial began almost two years later. (I had not returned to college, thinking I was briefly putting school on hold until the trial was completed.) I had three Scriptures in my heart that I was praying continually, although I don't even remember searching them out or being taught to confess them.

- *They shall know the truth and the Truth shall make me free* (John 8:32, my paraphrase).

- *If God be for me, who can be against me* (Romans 8:31)?

- *God causes all things to work for the good of those who love Him and are called according to His purpose* (Romans 8:28).

If I was awake, I was fervently praying and confessing these.

The trial was such a difficult experience! It was riddled with its own set of challenges. Jodie Foster's movie, *The Accused*, had been released not long before this and true to the film's message, rape **victims** were as much or **more** on trial than assailants (our character, our actions, our clothing, our very selves facing a trial of mindsets, stereotypes, and prejudice). I remember sitting in the courtroom while potential jurors were interviewed and hearing some of the extremely harsh opinions they expressed when cross-examined by the attorneys to assess their viability as potential jurors. One man was adamant that I had deserved whatever happened to me because I had been out at such a late hour of night, and **his** daughter would never be that foolish. Thank goodness, he was dismissed as a juror.

Also, the newspaper had erroneously reported statements I didn't make (that my assailant had black hair, pulled a knife on me, etc.) and I had to go through closed meetings with attorneys and judges to correct those misperceptions.

Something I didn't share with you earlier is that shortly before my maternal grandmother was murdered, she met with an attorney to ask advice about divorcing my grandfather. Divorce was discouraged during the Sixties, and he implored her to wait two weeks giving it another effort before making any hasty decisions. In taking his advice, she never lived through those two weeks! And as fate would have it (please note that I will soon be talking about our true enemy, and this was absolutely not a coincidence), my assailant had this same attorney as his defense attorney! In a closed meeting, I was explaining how I had actually told the authorities that the person who attacked me had stringy red hair, about the color of my mother's, and I took photos of my mother to show as an example. This attorney smugly commented, "Your mom has picked up a little weight, hasn't she?" (He also later shamelessly held my bra up in front of a courtroom of people after pulling it out of a manila envelope to ask if it was mine, as if there were several in the bushes where I was attacked. But I digress…)

At the completion of the trial, while waiting for the verdict, I was again passionately praying my three Scriptures. I had decided to wait in the Commonwealth Attorney's office for two reasons: if they found him guilty, I did not want to observe the painful reaction of his family members, and if he was acquitted, I couldn't face it in front of a crowd. My mom was there with me. I was pacing the floor, confessing my three scriptural mantras, and in a moment I will always vividly remember, Heaven met earth in my world.

I heard an audible Voice speak to me these words, "Don't worry, Child. He's guilty!" It was gentle, loud enough to be unmistakably heard without being overbearing, and FULL of a love and comfort beyond description. Every cell in my body responded to it immediately. I knew without an iota of doubt that it was **Jesus Christ**. My description of it was that this almost inconceivably beautiful and peaceful body of water

(He is the Living Water) had somehow taken an acoustic form and spoken on the inside of my ears straight into my heart where I was the only one who could hear it. The Voice had tone and vibrato and LIFE in it. I immediately began to cry happy tears, and my mother tried to comfort me, not yet knowing the reason for them. Within seconds of explaining it to her, we received news of the guilty verdict. It was several years later that I happened upon the Scripture in Revelation 14:2 that tells us *He has the Voice of many waters*, but that was my immediate overwhelming comparison upon hearing Him.

I also knew instinctively within me that the reason I was able to receive this communication from Heaven—from Jesus Himself—had something to do with my confessing the Scriptures I had held on to during the trial.

About five years later, my path crossed with a pastor and his wife who attended a Word of Faith church, and they consequently invited me. In attending this church, I was like a dry, parched sponge placed into water. It was as if veils were lifted from my eyes. Things started to make sense—my **life** started to make sense. The constant struggles I had faced began to have some logic to them because I learned not only a wealth of Truth about the God Trinity (Father, Son, and Holy Spirit), but the power within His Word, how to study and meditate His Word, ways to apply its power to my life, and the FACT that I had an enemy who had been trying rather successfully to screw things up for me and keep me in confusion about it.

Satan is Our Enemy

I'd like to make this as clear as possible: from birth—from conception even—each one of us has an enemy. He does not run around in red tights with horns or a pitchfork! And that exaggerated image of him gives him a frivolity he actually appreciates because it keeps him from being taken as seriously as he needs to be. It keeps mankind from realizing his diabolical and purely evil plot against each one of us. From his days in Heaven as an archangel created in splendor and glory to serve God to his treasonous attempts to overtake the Trinity which led to him being stripped of any grandeur and cast out with his demonic cohorts (one-third of the heavenly host), he has hated man. He has set himself against us **because** of God's great love for us. He is insanely, psychotically jealous of you and of me **because** God is wild about us. (We can read about this in 2 Peter 2 and Revelation 12.)

In actuality, God created the earth in magnificence and perfection for His most prized creation—the one who was not made just to please Him as the plants and animals did, but to be intimate with Him on a level above every other creation—**man**—made in His image. Everything He had brought forth by speaking His life-infusing, creative Word was good and perfect, and then *He **blessed** them* (Genesis 1:28). There was **no** curse—no imperfection, no lack, no sickness, no death, nothing negative of any kind. They **only** knew good. There was no knowledge of evil because there was no evil in their surroundings or circumstances to know about. He never intended for them to experience any amount of evil on any level. His intentions for them—for **us**—were positive, loving, and perfect from the beginning.

The current state of our increasingly used-up and dilapidated planet can be traced back to satan's initial lies and ensuing deception in the garden to Eve and then to Adam. When they listened and submitted to his influence, a curse—the Curse—entered the earth and has been in motion since then. They also inadvertently gave him the authority God had entrusted **to them** at creation. *And God said, Let Us (Father, Son, and Holy Spirit) make mankind in Our image, after Our likeness, and let* *them have **complete** authority...over all the earth and over everything that creeps upon the earth* (Genesis 1:26 $^{AMPC, AMP}$).

Satan had already been forcefully cast out of Heaven once and stripped of any power he possessed for his treason, but now he had access to man's authority through his deception and their sin to mess up everything! His weapon **is** deception, and he is expert at it! He has used his craftiness to his full advantage for centuries, eons to methodically wreak havoc. That's why Eve responded to God's question of what she had done with, *"The serpent (satan) [beguiled, cheated, outwitted, deceived, seduced] me"* (Genesis 3:13 ^{AMP}).

Why did he approach Eve in the garden? He is power-hungry but had lost his own authority and knew that God had given complete authority of the earth to mankind (not over Heaven, but over earth). He had wanted all power in Heaven when he sought to overthrow God but was willing to settle temporarily for this lesser authority in hopes of using it to eventually gain all control in Heaven and earth.

You can see in Job and other places in Scripture that he was even able to temporarily reenter the presence of God—the presence he had been cast out of—in man's place and authority until Jesus later *cleansed the Heavenlies with His own blood* (Job 1:6, Revelation 12:10, and Hebrews 9:11-26).

He is referred to throughout Scripture not only as satan, but also as the devil, a serpent, the accuser of the brethren, a murderer, a liar, the father of lies, the thief, a stumbling block, the tempter, a dragon, masquerader as an angel of light, the god of this world, and very specifically (1 Peter 5:8-9) as our **enemy** who *prowls around like a roaring lion seeking someone to devour*. And the third of Heaven who accompanied him in his treason are referred to as *principalities, powers, rulers of darkness of this world, and spiritual wickedness in high places* and attributed to being the reason we struggle in this life (Ephesians 6:12).

So what are we to do if we have an angry devil and his army determined to ruin our lives on any level they can? Realizing he is indeed our enemy is crucial to confronting and overcoming him! He is happy when people deny or downplay his existence. He is pleased when some don't even believe in God either or believe in false gods. He is thrilled when religion teaches that God has some aspects of both good and evil or even indifference toward man so that God becomes the scapegoat for man's problems. Any way that he can twist the truth gives him a deceptive advantage over us, even after being born again. Hosea 4:6 tells us *God's people are [being] destroyed for lack of knowledge*, and the ^{MSG} version goes on afterward to say *My people are ruined because they don't know what's right or true* and that the ministers who should be teaching Truth *have turned their backs on* [revelation] *knowledge* and *refuse to recognize* [or teach] *the revelation of God*.

But THANK GOODNESS God in His infinite wisdom and love for mankind has given us His eternal, creative Word and a measure of all the faith required to overcome satan (Romans 12:3), and the Trinity outnumbers him three to one. The angelic host are more numerous than his demons by two to one. He is a **creation**; God is **CREATOR**. We do not have to be afraid of him!

In fact, there are more than 365 times in the Bible that God instructs us not to fear and gives promises that counteract concern—one for every day of the year plus. The Bible even predicts in Isaiah 14:16-17 that we will someday *stare and muse at him, asking "Can this be the one who terrorized earth* and its inhabitants?" In other words, is this all he was? He is like the legendary and familiar little pipsqueak foe who just appears to cast a large and looming shadow.

But we **do** have to resist him and not fall for his lies and deception. Just as Peter warned us, and as 2 Corinthians 2:11 and several other Scriptures advise: *that Satan might not outwit us or get an advantage over us. For we are not unaware or ignorant of his schemes, wiles, and intentions.*

Even in his crafty brilliance, he has overplayed his hand to me so many times in so many obvious ways, some of which I've shared with you previously—how the **same** voice speaking the **same** words through different people has given me the **same** message for as far back as I can remember. He is almost as intricately and thoroughly detailed in his evil scheming as God is in His blessings to us. (Remember how I mentioned it was not just a coincidence when my attacker ended up with the same lawyer who had given my grandmother poor advice?)

There are countless times in my life I can see how satan was behind the scenes conspiring against me, and I now use this knowledge often to more readily recognize his attacks for what they are—shoddy attempts *to steal, kill, and destroy* (John 10:10)—and to resist him in his efforts. The voice that sometimes whispers and sometimes shouts to me to harm myself, to give up, and to quit is very easily attributable to him because he has blown his cover in his eager relentlessness to take me out. It reminds me of when the Wizard says, "Pay no attention to the man behind the curtain!" as he is trying to give off the façade of being large, looming, and intimidating to Dorothy and her friends (*Wizard of Oz* movie reference). Satan is the ultimate humbug.

Internalize God's Word—His Image of You

But being born again and realizing that satan is your mortal enemy are only first steps to overcoming your struggle with suicidal thoughts, or for that matter, anxiety or oppression of any kind. It is very important to let God's Word show you who you are in Christ and reveal to you how the Godhead sees you—and how you should see **yourself**. I've heard it said and completely concur that there is a spiritual blueprint within Scripture for each one of us. Colossians 3:3-4 ^{AMP} explains that *our real life—our true identity—is hidden with Christ in God*, and *as Christ is revealed to us, who we are created to be is revealed also*. In other words, as we study God's Word, and as we come to know more about Christ, we discover ourselves and His plans for us.

There are many Scriptures that pertain to all of us (example: John 3:16 which tells us of God's great love for the world and His desire that no one perish), and there are some Scriptures that do not apply to all of us (example: Isaiah 7:14 which discusses the virgin birth of Jesus).

This process of letting the Word show you who you are is exactly how Jesus came to know Himself after leaving Heaven to be born here on earth. From before the foundations of the earth, He was in Heaven as part of the Trinity, but He chose to lay aside His divinity and come to earth as a man, become the ultimate sacrifice for humanity, trade our sin and fallen nature for His righteousness, and become our redemption (Philippians 2:6-8).

Why was this necessary? Again, because **man** was given **complete** authority in the garden and then handed it over to satan by falling for his schemes and being disobedient, and it would take a **man** to get it back. Father God banished Adam and Eve from the garden to keep them from prematurely eating from the Tree of Life before Jesus could get here and fulfill His plan to fix things for us, which would have otherwise meant an eternity in a fallen state instead of an eternity in a state of salvation, restoration, and youth. And then God immediately began prophesying (using the creative force of His Word just like He had done in actually forming the planets) to set in motion our redemption (Genesis 3:15).

Everything reproduces after its kind, so from that point forward, every person would be born into that fallen state, subject to the Curse, just as their parents, Adam and Eve, were...until God could get a man to take back the authority which had been lost. That Man was Jesus, and as a man, He learned His identity by studying Scripture and letting the Holy Spirit teach Him who He was.

You see, even though He had been in Heaven before coming to earth, when He arrived, He wasn't a baby with an adult mind who automatically knew His identity and purpose—He had to find Himself within the Scriptures. He had to study the Word and let it reveal itself to Him—let it teach, shape, and prepare Him. He had to apply its guidance to His everyday life and build His image from the inside out. He had to mentally take in Scripture, meditate it, and let it get into His heart where it could really make a transformation in His life.

This is the same process I used to overcome the negative, paralyzing effects of all of the traumas I had faced in my life and my battles with low body image and self-esteem. I meditated and studied Scripture until it got on the inside of me.

Hebrews 4:12 tells us that the *Word of God is alive, powerful, and active*, and Jesus Himself said it is a seed to be sown to reap a harvest (Matthew 13:18, Luke 8:11). First Peter 1:23 adds that it is *an incorruptible seed which lives and abides forever*. Like a seed, it needs to be planted in favorable conditions, and it takes time to grow and produce the desired results. When we take in God's Word, it begins as head knowledge, as with any book we read or words on a page, and through meditation, thought, pondering, reflection and contemplation, its seed-like magic begins, and it starts to get down into our hearts and come up out of our mouths to yield life-changing results. Much like within natural seed, there is invisible life within it that doesn't become visible until planted and nurtured.

Quantity of Scripture is not the goal in this process, but rather, quality. Understanding all Scripture as a whole or all the mysteries of the universe isn't our goal either. First Corinthians 13:9-12 explains that in this earthly realm, *we know in part and see in part* but in Heaven *we shall know fully.* In other words, we don't have to understand the entire Bible to put its principles to work in our lives. Until we get to Heaven, there will be many general and personal questions we could ask and consequently risk getting hung up on in debate with others or even within ourselves.

For instance, I've often wondered why satan was cast to earth instead of immediately being banished to the lake of fire, or how Jonah survived in the belly of the whale without being digested. You may wonder why Aunt Suzie didn't receive her healing or why there is so much pain in the world if God's Word promises us otherwise. Scholars and the scientific community have long raised questions which result in confusion, like how the Bible seems to document seven thousand years while studies show our planet is possibly billions of years old. Or why there are so many religions in the world.

See how easy it can be to get bewildered with the perplexity of it all? And then we've talked ourselves right into a place of stagnancy that directly opposes our progress. So we must **choose** to put all of those unanswered questions on the back burner of our minds, and purposefully use what we **need** to make our lives better instead of trying to figure it all out.

When I'm struggling with my self-worth and hearing that suicidal whisper in my head, I don't really care how Jonah survived the whale or how old the planet is—I selfishly and wisely focus on what I need in my daily life to live by faith and run my race with grace. I trust that the rest will be explained later.

The Word of God is chock-full of promises for every need we could possibly have, and applying those specific scriptural promises to specific needs is the key to obtaining victory in each area of life. Just like with a natural garden, if we need potassium, we match up our crop accordingly by planting beets, yams, spinach, or pumpkin. If we want to increase our Vitamin C intake, we fill our garden with dark, leafy greens, broccoli, or bell peppers. There are scriptural promises for every need we face. Second Peter 1:3 says *God has given us all things pertaining to life and godliness.* That power is contained within His Word. Second Timothy 3:16-17 tells us that *every Scripture is God-breathed and inspired by Him and profitable for instructing, correcting, training, and teaching us so that we may be complete.*

I needed to be complete! I needed to have a more positive self-image right away! So just like my analogy of planting beets for potassium, I went to work planting God's Word of love for me in my heart as often as possible. I searched for Scriptures that told me amazingly beautiful and romantic ways He regards me. Scriptures such as Isaiah 62:3-5 that says *you will also be a crown of beauty in the hand of the Lord, a royal diadem, exceedingly beautiful in the hand of your God. It will no longer be said to you, "Forsaken," but you will be called, "My delight in in her," for the Lord delights in you, and as the bridegroom rejoices over the bride, so your God will rejoice over you.*

Oh my goodness! It no longer mattered how the boys in first grade or high school reacted to my affection. How my ex-husband had treated me in his insults and vile conduct was of no further consequence! The GOD OF THE UNIVERSE said I am exceedingly beautiful in **His** eyes. There is no one whose opinion matters more than His—whose estimation could affect my life over how He thinks of me—except maybe for me, myself. Holding on to this Word and letting it become my Truth was crucial, reinventing, life-giving, saving, and transforming. I literally even cut out pictures from magazines of ladies in wedding gowns, glued my face to their bodies, and framed it all up to get that image inside of me. I took the Scriptures I had found and recorded them to listen to during the day and while I slept, and I rehearsed them to myself more times than I could possibly begin to estimate.

And true to any seed, especially an incorruptible seed, it began to grow and change how I saw myself. I was being healed and strengthened day by day.

A Word(s) for Every Struggle

Just as I related earlier, the Word of God is overflowing with hundreds of promises that are just as much incorruptible seed as the Scriptures I used to gain a healthier self-image. They literally cover any need we could possibly ever have. Second Corinthians 1:20 makes an amazing claim that as *many as are the promises of God, they all find their Yes answer in Him (Christ), and for this reason we also utter the Amen (so be it)!* The ^{MSG} translation goes on to add *God's Yes and our Yes together* [make them] *gloriously evident...making **us** a sure thing in Christ, putting His Yes within us* [His incorruptible seed] *...a sure beginning of what He is destined to complete.* Seedtime and harvest.

In every area I have battled (each trigger previously mentioned), I have systematically used God's Word—specific promises for each deficiency—to plant that incorruptible seed toward the changes I needed to make for my life to not only feel survivable, but happy. For family struggles, I planted seeds of covenant for their peace and salvation. For work issues, I planted seeds that give me grace, favor, and wisdom. For medical issues, I planted seeds for healing. For sin issues, I plant seeds that lead me to repentance and promise forgiveness and righteousness.

And this Word grows—sometimes more quickly and sometimes more slowly—to make the improvements I need and to cause me to overcome in each of the areas in which I am challenged. But no matter how long it seems to take, *His Word never fails*, falls short, or lacks in its faithfulness to me (Isaiah 55:11 ^{GNT}, Joshua 21:45).

God is a God of covenant. In Ezekiel 16:60, He promises *I will remember My covenant with you in the days of your youth, and I will establish an everlasting covenant with you.* In Psalm 105:8 ^{AMPC}, Scripture promises that *He is earnestly mindful of His covenant and forever it is imprinted on His heart, the word which He commanded and established to a thousand generations.* Several Scriptures of the New Testament (new covenant) assure us that Jesus is our Covenant Mediator and that *the new covenant is established on better promises* (Hebrews 8:6).

Use Your Sword of the Spirit and Your Spiritual Armor

But just like within a natural garden, you have to be diligent about tending it. Remember what God said to Adam and Eve because of the Curse in the Garden of Eden? *The ground will sprout thorns and weeds; you'll get your food the hard way, planting and tilling the harvest, sweating in the fields from dawn to dusk* (Genesis 3:17-19 ᴹˢᴳ). No longer was the ground effortlessly producing bounteous harvests of fruit for the picking. Now it must be tended and cared for thoroughly to produce only what was desired.

If you've ever had any experience with a garden—whether vegetable or flower—you know that weeds are a given. You only plant what you want, and you would never think of planting weeds, but somehow they end up in your garden, vying for the sun, water, and nutrients your plants need to be successful and yield fruit. The **same** thing happens within the spiritual realm when you are planting God's Word for a harvest of His promises!

Jesus Himself said in a parable that *the kingdom of Heaven is like a man who sowed good seed in his field. But while everyone was sleeping, his enemy came and sowed weeds among the wheat, and went away. When the wheat sprouted and formed heads, then the weeds also appeared. The owner's servants came to him and said, 'Sir, didn't you sow good seed in your field? Where then did the weeds come from?' '****An enemy*** *did this,' he replied* (Matthew 13:24-28).

How does our enemy (satan) sow weeds into our potential harvests? Through his systematic lies and his attempts at deception. John 10:10 ᴬᴹᴾ makes it very plain that he is a thief—**the** *thief—who comes to steal, kill, and destroy, even though Jesus came to give us life, and not only life, but abundant life—to the full, until it overflows*. Have you heard of bumper crops? That's what Jesus desires for us!

So if satan is determined to sow weeds into our crops, how do we recognize and counteract them? Just as the seeds we are planting are words, the 'weed seeds' satan uses in his efforts to sabotage us are also in the form of words—they might be thoughts he puts into our heads that he hopes will eventually migrate to our hearts and out of our mouths to produce a negative harvest, or they could be verbal words someone else is speaking about us or to us, or things we hear, read, or see.

Fortunately, in the same chapter of Ephesians where we learn there are rankings within the demonic kingdom, Paul also teaches us about our complete spiritual armor to help us effectively counteract them!

> *Put on God's whole armor [the armor of a heavy-armed soldier which **God** supplies], that you may be able **successfully** to stand up against [**all**] the strategies and the deceits of the devil. For we are not wrestling with flesh and blood [contending only with physical opponents], but against the despotisms (principalities, rulers), against the powers, against [the master spirits who are] the world rulers of this present darkness, against the spirit forces of wickedness in the heavenly (supernatural) sphere. Therefore put on God's **complete** armor, that you may be able to **resist** and **stand your ground** on the evil day [of danger] and, having done all [the crisis demands], to stand [firmly in your place]. Stand therefore [hold your ground], having tightened the **belt of truth** around your loins and having put on the **breastplate of** integrity and of moral rectitude and right standing (**righteousness**) with God, and having **shod your feet** in preparation [to face the enemy with the firm-footed stability, the promptness, and the readiness produced by the good news] of the **Gospel of peace**. Lift up over all the [covering] **shield of** saving **faith**, upon which you can quench **all** of the flaming missiles (fiery darts) of the wicked [one]. And take the **helmet of salvation** and the **sword that the Spirit wields**, which is the **Word of God**. Pray at all times (on every occasion, in every season) in the Spirit, with all [manner of] prayer and entreaty* (Ephesians 6:11-18 [AMPC], emphasis added).

What an outfit God has provided for us! We hear that the clothes make the man or woman. How true in this instance. I heard a minister make the valid and tremendous point that when we are wearing God's armor, the devil doesn't know if he's battling us or Jesus! We look just like Him (made in His image), and we can be just as invincible as He is because we are using the weapons He's given us to **guarantee** our victory in Christ. He promises to *make us more than conquerors through Him Who loves us* (Romans 8:37).

Let's look at the individual pieces of the armor and how they help us:

•**Belt of Truth:** The Scripture says to have *your loins girt about with the belt of truth*. Loins are the expanse between our waist and pelvic area and, in references, imply a couple of connotations.

One association is that our loins are our core area which needs stabilizing for labor or battle, much as when a worker wears a back support for tasks which require heavy lifting or a soldier prepares to strap on his sword. The intent of the support is to provide extra stabilization and balance. We read earlier in Hosea 4:6 that God's *people are destroyed for lack of knowledge* and in John 8:32 that *if we know the Truth, it makes us free*. So metaphorically we are advised to wear truth as a girdle to equip ourselves with knowledge of God's Truth and to let that truth add balance, stability, and wisdom to our daily lives, direction, choices, and decisions—the core of who we are.

The truths and principles in God's Word should govern, guide, and control our every thought, conversation, and action. Peter echoes this when he says to *gird up the loins of our minds* in order to *be sober and* set our *hope upon the grace that comes to us with the revelation of Jesus Christ* (1 Peter 1:13 [KJV]). *So then, prepare your hearts and minds for action—as Jesus is unveiled, a greater measure of grace will be released to you* [TPT]! The more we know about the ways of God and the Word of God, the more grace we have.

The other implication to take from girding our loins is the association some Scriptures make with the loin area and reproduction. In Genesis 35:11 ^(KJV), God foretold to Jacob that *kings would come forth from his loins*. In Hebrews 7:5 ^(KJV), Scripture tells us that *the priests—the sons of Levi—came forth from the loins of Abraham*. So we see that God also views the belt of truth as a way to protect and channel our procreative, reproductive power, both in the spiritual realm (our authority as a believer) and the natural realm (our genetic offspring). Consider these two parallel verses:

> *I lavish unfailing love to a thousand generations. I forgive iniquity, rebellion, and sin. But I do not excuse the guilty. I lay the sins of the parents upon their children and grandchildren; the entire family is affected—even children in the third and fourth generations* (Exodus 34:7 ^(NLT)).

How often have we seen this? Children and grandchildren who are essentially born into struggle with odds stacked against them because of the sins of their fathers and grandfathers (or mothers and grandmothers)? It's a generational curse of sorts. How many struggles and addictions appear to have a genetic component?

But in contrast, we read in Proverbs 20:7:

> *The righteous man walks in his integrity; blessed (happy, fortunate, enviable) are his children after him* ^(AMP). *God-loyal people, living honest lives, make it much easier for their children* ^(MSG).

As we said earlier, everything reproduces after its kind, so if we walk in truth, having our loins girt about with the Truth of God's Word, we are making it easier for our children and grandchildren to also walk in truth.

Regarding our authority in the spiritual realm, it doesn't matter what our past family history may contain. Father God reproduces after His kind also. When we become a child of God, He empowers us to be *transformed into His image from glory to glory* (2 Corinthians 3:18 ^{NAS}). Truth applied in the correct context overrides generational curses, disadvantages, past sins, heredity, genetics, shortcomings, weaknesses, and *any created thing that would attempt to separate us from the love of God which is in Christ Jesus* as *our Lord* and *causes us to become more than conquerors* (Romans 8:37, 39).

Satan may have temporarily been able to keep us in a state where a lack of knowledge was working against us, but in girding ourselves with the Truth of God's Word and in understanding how His Kingdom works, we are able to wear this belt of truth effectively, accompanied with the other pieces of armor God has supplied, to become strong in the Lord and in the power of His might!

•**Breastplate of Righteousness:** This piece of our armor is of vital importance for the obvious reason that breastplates protect our hearts. Our faith goal in planting the seed of God's Word in our hearts is that within our hearts is the soil the Word needs to grow and manifest God's will and goodness in our lives. (Speaking from head knowledge is not where the authority and power lie, although this type of confession can be a preemptive and necessary step to aide in getting the Word rooted within our hearts.) It is the Word which has been meditated and nurtured deep within our hearts that is most powerful and productive!

That's what it took to be born again in Romans 10:10, when it said *with the heart we believe resulting in righteousness and* (then) *with the mouth confession is made unto salvation.* Proverbs 4:23 wisely tells us *to keep and guard our hearts with all diligence and vigilance,* **and above all that we guard** ^(AMP), *for out of it our very* *lives issue*. The ᴺᴸᵀ says *our heart determines the course of our life*, and the ᴹˢᴳ tells us *the heart is where life starts*. Proverbs 20:27 and similar Scriptures (Psalm 119:105, Proverbs 6:23, and many others) make it clear that our spirit man and our heart are intricately synonymous. It says *our spirit* (our heart) *is the lamp of the Lord*. God uses our spirits to make His ways and plans known to us to most effectively lead us. In other words, our heart is most often where we feel the promptings of the Spirit communicating to our spirits and, therefore, very essential to protect.

But this breastplate is more than just a heart covering. It is a breastplate of righteousness. Righteousness is defined as being free from guilt or sin, or more explicitly, free from the guilt **of** sin. The Bible references two types of righteousness: ours and Jesus's. Ours is produced by our good works, and His is earned by His sinless life. Ours is fallible, and His is faultless. Ours is lacking, and His is complete. Scripture says ours doesn't measure up to what we need to fully access God's goodness. Isaiah 64:6 says *we are all infected and impure with sin. When we display our righteous deeds, they are* (in comparison to the necessary standard) *nothing but filthy rags* ⁽ᴺᴸᵀ⁾. *We're all sin-infected, sin-contaminated. Our best efforts are grease-stained rags* ⁽ᴹˢᴳ⁾.

But, as is typical of God's divine, loving, and generous nature, He provides everything we need to walk victorious in life, including the VERY ADEQUATE righteousness of Jesus Himself. Possibly the greatest trade of all time. So much of the work Jesus did during His time here on earth was substitutionary.

He took our sickness so we could have His health. He took our sorrows and grief so we could have joy. He took our punishment for sin, actually went to hell for us during the three days between His crucifixion and resurrection to pay our sin debt, and gave us in exchange His salvation (Isaiah 53:5). He literally became sin so we could become His righteousness. *God made Him Who had no sin to be sin for us, so that in Him we might become the righteousness of God* (2 Corinthians 5:21).

After admonishing us not to worry about things such as food and clothing because if God so graciously provides those for the birds of the air and the flowers of the field, He will also provide them for us, Matthew 6:33 tells us to *seek first His kingdom and **His righteousness**, and all these things* (food, clothing) *will be given to us as well.* (Note that we are seeking His righteousness, not our own.)

How do we access this gift of righteousness? The same way we access our entire covenant: by faith. *But now apart from the law* (works), *the righteousness of God has been made known, to which the Law and the Prophets testify.* **This righteousness is given through faith in Jesus Christ to all who believe** (Romans 3:21-22). Again, *for in the Gospel the righteousness of God is revealed—a righteousness that is* **by faith** *from first to last, just as it is written: "The righteous will live by faith"* (Romans 1:17 [NAS]).

Adam lost our righteousness (along with our authority) in the garden through disobedience, but Jesus restored it to us by giving us His righteousness. *For just as through the disobedience of the one man the many were made sinners, so also through the obedience of the one Man the many will be made righteous* (Romans 5:19).

I've heard some ponder that the reason Adam and Eve were not aware of their nakedness in the garden is because they were actually clothed in righteousness before sinning. Interesting thought, for Isaiah 61:10 tells us that God clothes us in a robe of His righteousness, but even if that is accurate for pre-cursed Eden, clothing is still acceptable and recommended attire in most communities today (intentional humor). *I delight greatly in the Lord; my soul rejoices in my God. For He has clothed me with garments of salvation and arrayed me in a robe of His righteousness, as a bridegroom adorns his head like a priest, and as a bride adorns herself with her jewels* (Isaiah 61:10). Notice God is providing the robe, but we are adorning ourselves with it, by faith. That's a great connection to Matthew 6:28-33 referenced above where God promises to clothe us!

How powerful is this righteousness? Even though in his old man as Saul he had persecuted the Church before his encounter with Jesus on the road to Damascus (Acts 9:1-6), a solid revelation of His righteousness making us *a new creation in Christ Jesus* (2 Corinthians 5:17) allowed Paul to boldly say that he had *wronged no man* (2 Corinthians 7:2) and go on to write almost half of the New Testament to strengthen us in our faith.

Protecting our hearts with the breastplate of righteousness gives us a vital weapon to resist satan's condemnation and the strong assurance we need in prayer to receive from God. *Dear friends, if we don't feel guilty—if our hearts don't condemn us—we can come to God with bold confidence. And we will receive from Him whatever we ask because we obey Him and do the things that please Him* (1 John 3:21-22 NLT, KJV). *The prayer of a righteous person is powerful and effective* (James 5:16).

Whether you view it as a robe or a breastplate, righteousness (confidence in our Jesus-gifted rightstanding with God) is an essential component of our armor to protect our hearts and cause us to be most successful in our battle against satan.

•Feet Shod with the Preparation of the Gospel of Peace:
Every soldier also needs adequate protection for his feet. In ancient times when Paul wrote Ephesians, the shoes for a soldier to accompany an armor such as this were known as Caligae, rather odd-looking and interesting pieces of leather workmanship. They were heavy-duty, thick-soled openwork

boots that laced up the center of the foot and onto the top of the ankle. Being so open at the top seems like it would be more detrimental than beneficial, but the openwork lattice design allowed the feet to breathe which was cooler for the soldier while also preventing foot ailments. They as well contained hobnailed soles which functioned to give grip and foot-support and to serve as an additional weapon against foes. The soldier had to walk sometimes up to twenty-five miles per day and because of this, the overall design was helpful. I recently read, how long can anyone walk a hard and stony road without a decent pair of shoes? In parallel, we know life can be a hard journey to navigate.

Paul admonishes us to have our feet shod with the Gospel of peace *in preparation to face the enemy.* In commentaries I've read and sermons I've heard, often the association here is focused on evangelism, the Great Commission, and being ready to go into all the world and preach the Gospel (all noble and necessary endeavors), and this Scripture can loosely be applied in that context, but I think Paul had a much more personal meaning than that. He was teaching us to resist and withstand satan and his strategies and to firmly stand our ground during crisis—spiritual warfare, if you will. Each piece of armor has a very particular purpose to support us during battle. In other words, if I'm fighting for my life, this piece of armor helps me in a specific way in combat.

So what exactly did Paul mean? In looking back at the Greek etymology of each word within the phrase a deeper meaning emerges: have our feet shod (*to bind under one's feet, put on shoes or sandals*) with the preparation (*to prepare, provide, make ready, be in readiness, fitness, adjusted*) of the Gospel (*a good message, to announce good news, declare, bring glad tidings*) of peace (*prosperity, peace, quietness, rest, to set at one again*).

Satan will try to bring chaos as often as possible—constantly if he can—because he knows that it gives him an advantage and it is in direct opposition to the peace that God wants for us (James 3:16-17). He tries to bring confusion into our thoughts and circumstances and strife through other people to make our footing unsure and unsteady and to ultimately attempt to trip us up and disarm us.

But Jesus said *even though we encounter tribulation in the world, in Him we have peace, so we can be of good cheer* (John 16:33)! In John 14:27 ^{AMP}, He said, "*Peace I leave with you;* **My own peace** *I now give and bequeath to you. Not as the world gives do I give to you.* **Do not let** *your hearts be troubled,* **neither let** *them be afraid. [***Stop allowing yourselves*** to be agitated and disturbed; and* **do not permit yourselves** *to be fearful and intimidated and cowardly and unsettled.]*" The ^{MSG} adds, "*I don't leave you the way you're used to being left—feeling abandoned, bereft. So* **don't be upset. Don't be distraught**."

He makes it sound as if we have a choice? As if we can control our feelings and reactions? Yes! Exactly! Thinking back to the Caligae's hobnailed soles that provided stability and sure footing on unstable terrain and that served as an additional weapon against an enemy, consider Luke 10:19 ^{AMP}: *Behold! I have given you* **authority** *and* **power** *to trample upon serpents and scorpions, and [***physical and mental strength and ability***] over all the power that the enemy [possesses]; and nothing shall in any way harm you.* The ^{NLT} says we can *crush them*! (See also Genesis 3:15, Psalm 110:1, Romans 16:20.)

I was recently driving down the road preaching my peace covenant **to myself** reminding myself, God, and satan that the circumstances I was facing had to line up to the Truth of God's Word (2 Corinthians 4:18), and they did, but I had to be ready and prepared before the struggle happened so I wasn't overwhelmed and overturned by the junk going on around me contrary to my promises.

That's when it really dawned on me what Paul was saying: I had prepared myself beforehand through my prayer and study (**my feet were shod in preparation**) to walk out my peace covenant by confessing God's Truth and promise over the situation, preaching to myself, and reminding myself of the good news (**the Gospel of peace**) which overrides natural circumstances. King David did this also. He stirred himself up, preaching to himself, singing, reminding himself of the victories God had provided him in the past and of His faithfulness to him in their covenant (throughout Psalms, 1 Samuel 30:6).

Paul was saying that we can use our authority (the authority that Jesus regained for us) to crush the enemy and walk in peace, the God kind of peace that prospers us and sets us at one again so that we may **rest** in our covenant even in the midst of combat. We can **overcome** and rest through having our feet shod and protected. **Protected** by being prepared and fit, ready before we need it, ready before the battle begins. **Ready** to remind ourselves of the good news, to **announce** and **declare** to ourselves (and satan) the glad tidings that we have a covenant of peace with our covenant God which **guarantees** us victory over every circumstance and situation that arises. We have to be prepared to walk it out, prepared to walk out our covenant of peace and trample satan underfoot! How do we apply this? In conjunction with each of the other pieces of armor. Keep reading.

•**Shield of Faith:** Paul places special emphasis on this part of our armor when he tells us to *lift it above all*. He says that with it we *can quench all* (yes, **all**) *the fiery darts of the evil one* (satan). This is an extremely powerful statement! (Not nine out of ten. Not ninety-nine out of a hundred. All.)

So then, what is faith? In its simplest terms, it is believing in something—taking God at His Word. Webster's says it is complete trust. First Thessalonians 3:7 ᴬᴹᴾᶜ explains faith as *the leaning of our whole personality on God in complete trust and confidence*.

But biblical faith is so much more than that. It is an unseen spiritual force, much like gravity is an unseen physical force. We know that gravity holds us onto the planet and keeps us from being sucked out into the universe even though earth is rotating at a constant speed of over a thousand miles per hour, and gravity works even though we can't visibly see or tangibly touch it. As well, the law of gravity is in operation regardless of who believes it.

Similarly, the spiritual force of faith is at work regardless of whether we are aware of it. Faith is a spiritual law like gravity is a physical law. Faith is our access point to receive from God. It is the currency within His kingdom. In essence, faith in His Word is how His kingdom operates—how we bring *days of Heaven* to earth (Deuteronomy 11:21, Matthew 6:10) and manifest God's good plans for our lives (Jeremiah 29:11). If you can believe it, you can receive it (Mark 11:24). If you can build your faith for it, you can have it (conditional, of course, to "it" being a covenant promise which lines up to His Word and His will for you).

Remember that God created this planet for us, His most precious creation, and there was no sickness, no lack, no want or need of any kind which wasn't already provided—until the Curse entered. Consequently, there is no lack of any kind in Heaven right now. Several Scriptures tell us that God has provided everything we need to live an abundant life. Faith reaches over into the spiritual realm and hooks what we need so that we can reel it into our lives. As we discussed before, when we plant the seed of God's Word, our faith is what causes it to yield a harvest, *some thirty, some sixty, some hundred-fold* (Matthew 13:8) in varying levels determined by the strength and endurance of our faith.

Hebrews 11:1 *AMP* says that *faith is the assurance (the confirmation, the title deed, and substance) of things hoped for and the proof and evidence of things we do not yet see—the conviction of their reality even though they are not yet revealed to our senses.* In other words, faith believes we have something based on God's promise before our eyes can actually see it. We "see" it with our eyes of faith in our hearts first while the spiritual force of faith is working to manifest it in our lives.

Can something invisible really create visible benefits for us? Verse 3 adds that *everything we see was created by what we can't see*, referring to the spiritual realm and God calling and speaking the universe into existence with His Word. Other verses in this chapter—known by some as the faith Hall of Fame—go on to tell of men and women of faith taking God at His Word to overcome great obstacles, perform mighty acts, and receive personal victories in their circumstances against impossible odds.

Just one example of this is in verse 7 where *Noah, being warned by God about things **not yet seen**, prepared an ark to save his family* and preserve mankind. Noah received a Word from God, placed his faith in it, put consistent God-led action with it (James 2:17 *AMPC*), and overcame conditions that destroyed all of those without faith even though he had never before seen rain. He literally took God at His Word and trusted Him to his benefit and the benefit of his family—and ultimately to all future generations of mankind (you and me).

Second Corinthians 4:18 tells us *not to look at the things which are seen but the things which are unseen because the things which are seen are temporary but the things which are unseen are eternal.* In other words, our faith can change natural circumstances and cause them to line up with eternal truths regardless of what things currently look like. And that faith is the proof, the title deed, that it is already ours, sooner or later manifesting in reality in our lives.

We initially receive a *measure of faith* from God (Romans 12:3). This spiritual force of faith is much like a muscle. It can be developed and strengthened. Romans 10:17 tells us that *faith comes by hearing* (receiving) *the Word of God*. When we read or hear God's Word, it causes a hope to rise up within us that results in increased faith. Receiving the Truth of God's Word through meditation, study, preaching that we hear, or some other means is like weightlifting for our spirits. It makes deposits into our spiritual faith accounts. It pumps up our spirit man. It builds our faith which in turn helps us access God's covenant promises in greater measure (thirty, sixty, hundred-fold) and helps us shield ourselves from the onslaughts of satan.

God desires that we *live by faith* (Romans 1:17)—and unlike the religious connotation of this where we picture someone living from paycheck to paycheck and barely getting by—faith actually causes us *to be fully agreeable to God* or fully able to line up to how His kingdom operates in order to receive the ample covenant promises He sincerely desires for us (Romans 8:32, Luke 12:32). He is truly *a rewarder of those who diligently seek Him* (Hebrews 11:6)! Working to develop a strong faith allows us to more completely walk in the authority and blessing that Jesus has restored to us. Remember, Jesus Himself said that He has *come to give us abundant life to the full until it overflows* (John 10:10), and 1 John 5:4 says that our *faith is the victory that overcomes* and conquers *the world*.

Thus, Paul placed such an emphasis on the shield of faith—*lifting it above all*—because, along with God's Word, it is **essential** to how the entire kingdom of God works, and it is our access point to everything God desires for us. Moreover, the other pieces of armor only work when we place faith in them.

※

•**Helmet of Salvation:** Learning to wear our helmet of salvation is of critical importance in battling suicidal thoughts! It is central to our Christian walk as well. Its importance **cannot** be overstated. A helmet's purpose is to protect our heads, and our heads are where we do our thinking.

I recently heard a minister say that wearing our helmet of salvation is learning to think like a person who is saved. There is truth in this. Especially when we consider that the biblical word often translated as "saved" in the New Testament has a very amazing meaning in the Greek language. It is the word **sozo** (Strong's Concordance *4982*), and it literally means *to save, deliver, protect, heal, preserve, do well, be (make) whole*. It is parallel to the Old Testament Hebrew word, **shalom** (Strong's Concordance 7965), which most accurately means *happy, friendly, welfare, health, prosperity, peace, safety, favor, rest, all is well, perfect, whole*.

As you can see, much of its intended meaning, which can be summarized as *nothing missing or broken, whole, complete*, has been lost in translation, so as we learn to think like a person who is saved, we expand that limited definition in our hearts and minds to include so much more than salvation alone; and those expanded parameters then begin to include not only salvation, but health and healing, protection, provision, deliverance, general well-being and welfare, empowerment—a covenant greater than we've previously dared to imagine or realize from the limited perspective we knew prior. And these all-inclusive salvation thoughts are what we must protect, defend, and guard with our helmet.

The Bible has much to say about our thoughts, and thoughts are located within our minds—our souls.

You see, we are triune beings (1 Thessalonians 5:23, Hebrews 4:12). We have three distinct parts which make us up (similar to Father, Son, and Holy Spirit being triune). We are a spirit—this is our true self—the part of us that will live forever, even after we leave this natural realm. Our spirit is designed to be led by the Holy Spirit to make our lives most successful (Galatians 5:16, 25). As the saying goes, "We are not human beings having a spiritual experience—we are spiritual beings having a human experience."

Another part of us is our body. The Bible often refers to it as our flesh. It is our "earth suit" that keeps us anchored to this natural realm. It is genetically carnal and fallen since the garden. It has an insatiable appetite and can, when unrestrained, lead us in directions we later regret. Our flesh is usually inclined to want to be lazy and set itself against wisdom. For example, it typically wants to eat, drink, or sleep too much, spend too much money, or many other impractical or even harmful things. Our flesh can be very addictive by nature and is easily hooked on anything we consume in excess.

Closely connected to our spirit man is our soul. It consists of our mind, will, and emotions. It is basically the six or so inches between our ears. God intended for our minds to garner both worldly intelligence (common sense, education, fields of specialty) and spiritual wisdom (found in His Word). Our will is meant to be a strength to us because when we learn to properly use willpower, we can add stability to our choices and our lives. The willpower of man has accomplished great things! Add God to our willpower, and our potential is exponentially increased. Our emotions are meant to bless us, as we feel and experience love and goodness in our lives, but emotions can easily get out of hand, if not disciplined. (We all know people who seem to live on a rollercoaster of emotion, up one day and down the next (and we've been there too), or they wear their hearts on their sleeves, or react rashly in situations, in essence being controlled by their feelings.)

Our souls decide whether to side with our spirits and do the things that are beneficial to us and pleasing to God or to give place to our emotions or our flesh. Romans 8:6 says *for to be carnally minded is death* (because it pursues sin or excess) *but to be spiritually minded is life and peace* (the spiritual well-being that comes from walking with God). This verse explains that our souls either pair up with our spirits or our flesh. [Spirit + soul] = [spiritually minded]. [Flesh + soul] = [carnally minded].

Again, God designed our spirits to lead us. Our souls should filter our thoughts and emotions and decide actions which benefit us. Our flesh is to be subject to and tamed by our spirits and souls. In other words, spirit first, soul second, flesh last.

The helmet of salvation refers to the soul part of us. (We can say that its sole purpose is to protect our souls.) The soul is where most of our battles are fought. It is the gateway or conduit through which satan most frequently attacks us, other than physical attacks such as illness or outside circumstances. The only way he can gain access to our spirits is through our souls, through our thoughts. *The fiery darts of the enemy* the Bible refers to **are** thoughts (Ephesians 6:16)!

We are bombarded with thoughts all day and night, every single day. They may be directed at us or generalized. They may come through spoken words or things we read. They may originate from outside sources, such as other people, social media, news, radio, television, movies, music, public places, or sometimes they seem to develop right inside our own minds.

What many people don't realize is that those kinds of thoughts (the ones we think we thought of ourselves) don't always originate within us. If a thought enters my mind without obvious outside source, I must consider whether it is from God, from myself, or from satan because thoughts within our minds come in monotone.

If I audibly hear words spoken from someone, I can distinguish the timbre of the voice and use that to determine the identity and origination of the resulting thoughts. (For instance, I can recognize the voice of a friend as soon as she speaks without even seeing her.) But if the thought is inside my head without intonation, I lose the advantage of the distinction within the voice quality to determine its source.

And one of satan's easiest and most successful tricks is to shoot a thought into our minds that he doesn't take credit for. He wants us to think that his destructive and negative thoughts are actually our own! He will not say, "This is satan, and I am sending you this thought." He will throw the thought at us, using the "me, myself, and I" pronouns we use in reference to ourselves (*I feel so hopeless...I feel like I can't go on...*), and stand back to see if we will assume that we thought of it and take ownership of it. Why? Because it's easier for him to sell us on thoughts if we don't know he sent them. If we knew they were from him, we'd be more likely to reject them, just as you'd reject and return a delivery that you didn't want or order.

For years I listened to him plant negative and destructive thoughts within my head that he spoke through others (the consistent voice that seemed to speak the same message through various people throughout my life) and that were whispered within my own head—thoughts he tricked me into taking as my own. Thoughts of inadequacy and unworthiness in my appearance and my general self. Worries. Insecurities. Doubts. Fears. Temptations.

How can we battle this sophisticated level of deceit? As I said before, the Bible gives us very clear instruction on our thought life, as we saw earlier when Paul advised us to be spiritually minded (Romans 8:6). Romans 12:2 warns us *not to be conformed to this world*—not to think the way it thinks or act the way it acts. The [NLT] says to *let God transform you into a new person by changing the way you think. Then you will learn to know God's will for you, which is good and pleasing and perfect.* I'll repeat, we learn to think like a person who is saved (*sozo*ed).

Ephesians 4:23-24 ^{NLT, NIV} also tells us to *let the Spirit renew our thoughts and attitudes* and to *put on our new nature, created to be like God, in His image of righteousness and holiness.* Colossians 3:2 says to *set our minds and keep them set on things above*, to think about the things of Heaven, not the things of earth—to see things from Christ's perspective. Does this mean to keep our heads in the clouds? So heavenly minded that we're of no earthly good like some of the fanatical Christians who make the news? It doesn't mean that at all! It means to think the way God thinks about ourselves and our circumstances. It's what I did with my vision board when I reprogrammed my thinking to line up with God's thoughts about me instead of the lies I had continually heard.

My grandmother had an old metal sieve she used for straining liquid from foods she'd cooked. It separated what she wanted to keep from what she wanted to get rid of. I often envision the helmet of salvation like that old sieve she used, allowing thoughts we want and straining out thoughts we need to discard. It's what 2 Corinthians 10:5 ^{AMP, MSG} tells us to do when it says we should *refute arguments and theories and reasonings* (no matter their source) *that set themselves up against the* true *knowledge of God* (what we know He truly wants and thinks for us), *fitting every loose thought and emotion and impulse into the structure of life shaped by Christ, bringing every thought captive to Christ.* We have to keep a tight rein on our thoughts and emotions because loose thoughts that are allowed to bounce around in our minds counteract and threaten our well-being. Specifically, we are making our thoughts line up to God's Word and refusing thoughts that don't, no matter how they originated or who authored them. In conjunction with our sword of the Spirit, using our helmet of salvation works like this:

- **Recognize the lie:** I am ugly. Everyone thinks so.
- **Cast down and reject the lie:** I cast that thought down in Jesus' Name!
- **Replace the lie with Truth:** *I am exceedingly beautiful in the hand of my God* (Isaiah 62:3)! *I have the incorruptible beauty of a gentle and quiet spirit which is precious in God's sight* (1 Peter 3:4)!

Any negative thought, any thought that makes us feel defeated or discouraged (especially that makes us disparage life itself), any thought that contradicts what God's Word proclaims as Truth, must be replaced with corresponding Scripture that counteracts it. Why is this process so important? Because *as a man thinketh* **in his heart**, *so is he* (Proverbs 23:7). Thoughts that get **past our souls** go to **our hearts**, where our faith is. This can be helpful if good thoughts are building our faith, but destructive if negative thoughts are left unchecked and hinder our faith.

Think back to the analogy that Jesus Himself made of the garden, where the sower sows the Word, and the enemy attempts to sow weeds among the crop to strive against the desired harvest (Matthew 13:28). Just as in a natural garden, weeds compete for the nutrients and water the intended crop needs. In Mark 4:14-20, a similar parable tells how *satan comes immediately, as soon as the Word is sown, to try to take it away*, or to eventually *choke it out with cares, worries, troubles, and difficulties*. His ammunition, his seeds of doubt, are thoughts, and we must use the process described above (identifying lies, casting them down, replacing them with Truth) to weed out his influence in our thought lives in order to guard the fertile soil of our hearts and protect our faith.

This is why Philippians 4:8 [AMP] admonishes us that *whatever is true, whatever is worthy of reverence and is honorable and seemly, whatever is just, whatever is pure, whatever is lovely and lovable, whatever is kind and winsome and gracious, if there is any virtue and excellence, if there is anything worthy of praise, think on and weigh and take account of these things [fix your minds on them].* Meditate on them.

It is worth repeating in the ᴹˢᴳ for emphasis: *Summing it all up, friends, I'd say you'll do your best by filling your minds and meditating on things true, noble, reputable, authentic, compelling, gracious—the best, not the worst; the beautiful, not the ugly; things to praise, not things to curse.*

In order to recognize satan's negative thoughts, we need to be familiar with our covenant privileges; we need to understand how God truly feels about us; and we need to know what the Word says, in general and specifically toward us. We need to be aware of the greater Truth to be able to identify and refute his lies. It is much easier for us to replace thoughts than to try to stop thinking them. Wearing the helmet of salvation to filter our thoughts through the lens or sieve of God's Word and perspective can make all the difference to our esteem and well-being!

•**Sword of the Spirit:** The last piece of our armor is, as Paul told us at the end of Ephesians 6:17, *the sword of the Spirit—which is the Word of God.* We have already considered the Word as our seed in the parable of the sower, as Jesus shared in the Gospels. Although the Word can manifest quickly when we sow it, in general, seedtime and harvest suggest a process—a time of waiting, watering, and weeding before we reap the fruits and benefits of our labor.

In addition to being seed, the Bible makes other connections to the Word that are important to know in considering it as, not only a process manifesting good in our lives, but an immediate defense against our ultimate enemy—satan. John 1:1-3 tells us that *Jesus **is** the Word made flesh,* that *the Word was present at the beginning of time* (we know this from Genesis 1 where we saw that God spoke everything into existence), and that *everything that was created came into being through the Word*. Verse 14 says *the Word became human flesh and dwelt among us* (until the crucifixion). In other words, Jesus is the Word of God made into a Man. This is so complex yet so simple. (I love knowing that when I read, meditate, or speak a Word from Scripture, I am not only feeding my spirit, planting powerful seed, and building my faith, but I am embracing Jesus Himself.)

Hebrews 1:3 [AMP] tells us that *the entire physical and spiritual universe is upheld (maintained, guided, and propelled) by His mighty Word of power*. These truths are mirrored in Colossians 1:16-17 [AMP], *for by Him all things were created in Heaven and on earth, visible and invisible...all things were created and exist through Him and for Him. And He Himself existed and is before all things, and in Him all things hold together. [His is the controlling, cohesive force of the universe.]*

A word of caution here: religion has long held and taught the false belief from Scriptures like those above that God is in control of everything that happens and so, everything—good and bad—must be part of His plan and will. This is absolutely not true and not what those verses are saying. A few quick examples (as well as countless Scriptures) can disprove this flawed theology.

Think back to man's fall in the garden—everyone was hence forth separated from God and hell-bound. If God had been in control of that situation and it was part of His plan and will for mankind to be separated from Him, there would have been no need for a Saviour to reconcile us to Him. He would have had us right where He wanted us. We would just go to hell, lost without His intervention. But instead, 2 Peter 3:9 tells us that *the Lord is **not willing** for any to perish but that **all** should come to repentance* (the exact opposite of the situation in Genesis). It is **not** His will for any to face eternity apart from Him (even though, sadly, some shall).

And what about the often-heard question of why God allows people to be hungry all over the world? Is He both good and evil? Is this part of His will? Actually, according to Scripture, **we** are allowing this. In several Scriptures (Proverbs 19:17, 22:9, 25:21, Isaiah 58:7, 10, Luke 3:11, James 2:15-16, 1 John 3:17), we are asked to feed the poor as the body of Christ (1 Corinthians 12:27), the hands and feet that He works through, and promised as we do this, we are doing it *unto Him* (Matthew 25:35-45).

Another example is on a more personal level. How many times when tragedy or misfortune strikes us closer to home do we hear that it must be part of God's will or plan? For instance, when my grandmother was brutally murdered by her husband who was supposed to protect and cherish her, a misinformed minister told an eleven-year-old boy—my uncle—who had witnessed this crime against his mother that it was all part of God's plan somehow and that God was in control. That lie has perpetuated the pain and isolation he has felt for years because how do you turn to or trust a god who operates like this?

I have sat in congregations where I've heard members give testimonies about God that were way off base, like the man who praised God for breaking his leg to make him slow down and spend more time with Him. I've listened to people attempt to console others reeling from the tragedy of losing a loved one by telling them God wanted another flower in His garden or some other false explanation.

While attending a funeral service for a student's mother who had died from a drug overdose, I heard a minister tell those present how her addiction was a blessing in disguise because it had brought her closer to God, and that He gives His toughest battles to His strongest soldiers, as if God gave her that addiction or it was part of His plan for her life. Her seven-year-old son was sitting next to me.

This is not a valid representation of the character of God. His love is not two-faced or evil in any way. In fact, Hebrews 1:3 also tells us that Jesus is *the very image of God's nature* (AMPC), *the express image of His Person* (KJV), Who *perfectly mirrors God* (MSG), and is *a perfect imprint of His Father's essence* (AMP). Based on this Truth, we can read through the Gospels and see in Jesus, in His words and actions, exactly what the heart of the Father is and what He is truly like.

This flawed theology fails to include that we have an enemy who is thrilled for God to be the scapegoat for the problems **he** causes mankind. Acts 10:38 (AMP) tells us that *Jesus was anointed by God* (reflecting the heart of God) *with strength, ability, and power to go about doing good and healing* **all** *who were harassed, oppressed, and beaten down* ***by the devil****, for God was with Him.* This tells us that satan was behind the problems these people faced. Did they see him working within their lives? No. They saw his results—blind eyes, deaf ears, leprosy, poverty, sin—but satan was causing their problems.

Jesus (the essence of the Father) wanted to heal them **all**, if they were willing to come to Him. First John 3:8 (AMPC) tells us that the **very *reason*** *Jesus came* to earth *was to undo, destroy, loosen, and dissolve the works the devil has done* to us. The devil is the enemy to mankind. In Christ, we have victory over him.

So then, seeing that God's will is **not** evil toward us, and that His heart favors us, now let's look at what His plan and will **are**: *For I know the plans and thoughts I have for you, says the Lord, plans for peace and well-being and not for disaster, to give you a future and a hope* (Jeremiah 29:11). Remember that as we renew our minds, we are able to discern and *prove what His good, acceptable, and perfect will is* toward us (Romans 12:2). If you hear a doctrine, sermon, or viewpoint contrary to this, steer clear! Don't buy these religious lies!

So what are those verses meaning then, when they say *the entire universe is created and upheld by the Word of His power*? Just as we said, God spoke everything into existence, and set into motion physical and spiritual laws which keep everything running (planets rotating, *seedtime and harvest* functioning, *days and nights, seasons*, etc.) *as long as the earth remains* (Genesis 8:22). He also spoke prophesies to frame events, some that have come to pass, and many that are being fulfilled now and in the future. But the day to day of our lives is very much up to us, and our faith can shape our individual worlds. That's why Paul instructed us to use our armor in the first place—to defeat the thief and lay hold of the abundant life Jesus came to provide us (John 10:10).

Hebrews 4:12 tells us that *the Word of God is alive and active, full of power (operative, energizing, and effective) and is sharper than any two-edged sword*. Psalm 138:2 says *God has exalted and magnified His Word together with (and above) His name*. The [NLT] says that *His promises are backed by all the honor of His name*. That's because He's faithful to His covenant with us.

God told Jeremiah that He Himself *actively watches over His Word to perform it* (Jeremiah 1:12). The [MSG] says *I'm sticking with you. I'll make every Word I give you come true*. God told Isaiah that His Word *does not return void without accomplishing what He desires and succeeding and prospering in the matter for which He sends it* (Isaiah 55:11). The [NLT] says it *always produces fruit where it is sent*.

Psalm 103:20 [NAS] declares *bless the Lord, you His angels, who excel in strength, to perform His commandments and carry out His plans*, heeding to and *obeying the voice of His Word*. (Did you catch that?) The angels obey the **voice** of God's Word. When we are **speaking** and giving **voice** to His Word in faith, they work for us to bring it to pass. Hebrews 1:14 [NAS, AMP] tells us that, in fact, angels are *ministering spirits* whose purpose is to *protect us* and *render service* for us as part of our inheritance.

Daniel saw this Truth in action when an angel visibly appeared to him during a time of prayer and fasting over prophetic words God had given to Daniel, and the angel declared to him that *he had come in response to his* (Daniel's) *words* (Daniel 10:12).

Can we do this? Can we speak God's Word and expect angels to act on it and God Himself to back it up? Emphatically, YES! Again, that's what seedtime and harvest is all about as the sower sows the Word. Jesus Himself gave us that parable, and He referred to the sower in plural when He said, these are **they** who varied from having the Word taken from them to reaping hundredfold (Mark 4:15-20). He intends for us to receive the Word, sow it, tend it, and reap its benefits! That's what Father God has been doing with His prophetic voice since the garden of Eden—sowing His Word about Jesus and His beloved creation to obtain the harvest He desires in us. This is also similar to what using our sword of the Spirit means. It's what Paul meant when he wrote in 2 Corinthians 4:13 (referencing Psalm 116:10 AMP), *yet we have the same spirit of faith as he had who wrote in Scripture, I BELIEVED, THEREFORE I SPOKE. We also believe; therefore, we also speak.*

Romans 10:8 AMPC, AMP says that *the Word is near us, in our mouths, on our lips, and in our hearts—the Word of faith*. Not only **can** we speak it, but we **should be** speaking it! It's a covenant privilege. The MSG says that *the Word that saves is right here, as near as the tongues in our mouths, as close as the hearts in our chests*. Remember all that *saves* encompasses (health and healing, protection, salvation, prosperity, etc.). It's the Word of faith that welcomes God to go to work and set things right for us, and according to Psalm 103:20, it gives the angels their directives also. Matthew 12:34-35 says *from the abundance of the heart, the mouth speaks and brings forth what is good* (*season after season* MSG). Proverbs 18:21 says *death and **life** is in the power of the tongue, and those who love it will eat its fruit.*

How does the sword of the Spirit protect us? When we speak God's Truth—a Scripture—in response to a thought we've taken captive or a situation contrary to our covenant of peace, as we saw in learning to wear our helmet of salvation, we are using the Word of God as a sword to divide lie from Truth and defend ourselves. Using God's Word as a sword is not the same as sowing it. It is more confrontational, a defensive battle strategy.

When I was using my vision board and renewing my mind through meditation, I was planting and sowing God's Word as a seed for a specific harvest of a healthy self-image.

When I did the lie replacement in the midst of an onslaught of negative thoughts (identifying lies, casting them down, replacing them with Truth), I was using the Word as my sword of the Spirit to immediately resist satan and overcome those thoughts. (Both are important and Word-based.)

It is exactly what Jesus did when He was tempted of satan in the wilderness. Every time satan tempted Him with anything, His response was, *"It is written,"* and He quoted an appropriate Scripture against satan to resist and defeat his attack (Matthew 4:4, 7, 10, Luke 4:4, 8, 12). James 4:7 promises that if we will *submit to God and resist the devil, he will flee from us*. Choosing to believe and speak His Word in the face of an attack is submitting ourselves to God and using our sword to resist satan, by faith. It is bringing the living, active, powerful Word of God (remembering that Jesus Himself is the Word) onto the scene to battle for us. *This is the victory that overcomes the world, even our faith* (1 John 5:4).

※

Just as Paul declared, each part of the armor effectively worn together allows us to **successfully** *stand up against **all** the strategies and the deceits of the devil* (Ephesians 6:11 [AMPC]). As the [MSG] says in reference to the same passage (Ephesians 6:14-17) about our spiritual armor,

Be prepared. You're up against far more than you can handle on your own. Take all the help you can get, every weapon God has issued, so that when it's all over but the shouting, **you'll still be on your feet**. *Truth, righteousness, peace, faith, and salvation are more than words. Learn how to apply them. You'll need them throughout your life.* **God's Word is an indispensable weapon**.

Make Covenant With Others Who Can Intercede For and With You

Another important component of battling suicidal thoughts is being willing to open up about what we're feeling. This takes courage and must be done with care. Unfortunately, the precedent set in our current society is that for the most part, we don't talk about it. It is a taboo subject for many reasons, and by the time we get to the point when we share our feelings, we're often in a critical condition. (Any time that we feel completely hopeless to the point of being a danger to ourselves, we should reach out immediately to someone in a position to help us, whether through 911, a crisis line, a therapy center, a pastor, a trusted family member or friend, or someone nearby. The inset page of this book contains important contact information you may find helpful during a crisis.)

On the flip side of this, we typically shouldn't discuss it with just anyone or everyone. Not everyone is trustworthy, and some of the people in our direct circumstances are the very people whose actions have contributed to our feelings in the first place. Toxic people often have no remorse or positive, supportive response to a revelation that they are hurting someone else. They deflect, generalize, or rationalize their behaviors to lessen any need for guilt on their parts and, therefore, usually aren't willing or reliable to help us.

And not everyone, however well-intentioned or loving toward us, is capable of handling conversations of such content. For example, I remember when I used to tell my son how I was feeling in an effort to get him to examine his actions to me; my hope was that he would realize that his choices and the anger he was directing at me were causing me a huge amount of pain, but he thought I was threatening suicide to manipulate him, and he had no idea how to proactively respond or help me. Within his own struggles and because of his youth, he lacked the ability to empathize or assist me in mine.

I am a social person and have a lot of people in my life whom I consider friends, but I seldom share my battles outside of my inner circle of covenant relationships because in sharing, I need someone to add their faith with mine, not to multiply worry or concern by criticizing, doubting, or becoming fearful on my behalf, which could counteract or hinder my progress. Scripture wisely advises us not to *team up with those who are unbelievers* (without faith) (2 Corinthians 6:14 ^{NLT}). The ^{AMP} says to not *make mismated alliances inconsistent with our faith*. In other words, I have to use discretion and prudence with whom I trust with thoughts of this weight. This doesn't mean I withhold my friendship, but I am wise about sharing my innermost struggles.

Because we don't know who to reach out to, or we've reached out to some who lacked the capability to help us, suicidal thoughts can be very isolating; and isolation, loneliness, and seclusion are some of the strategies satan wants to use against us. **But God does not want us to be alone in our struggles!** He wants us to be able to break out of isolation and to have covenant partners in our lives with whom we can exchange godly counsel, wisdom, and advice. He will give us people we can lock hands and hearts with in effective prayer.

If we ask Him and trust Him, God will place people within our lives to mentor us and exchange wisdom with us when we need it. They won't necessarily have the same struggles we have, but they will need us and benefit from our prayers too. The covenant relationships that God has given me—people whom I can call upon to stand with me in my trials and challenges—are rare and precious. Through our joint prayers for each other, we've seen miracles, comfort, solutions, and wisdom manifest in one another's lives.

The ^{MSG} passage from Ephesians 6:14-17 that we looked at in the last section regarding our spiritual armor goes on to say after telling us that God's Word is our indispensable weapon,

> *In the same way, prayer is essential in this ongoing warfare. Pray hard and long. Pray for your brothers and sisters. Keep your eyes open. Keep each other's spirits up so that no one falls behind or drops out* (verse 18).

Galatians 6:2 ^{AMP} says to *carry one another's burdens and in this way you will fulfill the requirements of the law of Christ [that is, the law of Christian love]*. Ecclesiastes 4: 9-10, 12 ^{NLT} says *two people are better off than one, for they can help each other succeed. If one person falls, the other can reach out and help. But someone who falls alone is in real trouble. A person standing alone can be attacked and defeated, but two can stand back-to-back and conquer. Three are even better, for a triple-braided cord is not easily broken.* The ^{MSG} says that *it's better to have a partner than to go it alone; by yourself, you're unprotected. With a friend you can face the worst. Can you round up a third? A three-stranded rope isn't easily snapped.*

Having loyal prayer partners gives us an advantage over our enemy, satan, when he attacks. There is such power in covenant partnership and in the prayer of agreement! Jesus Himself said in Matthew 18:19, *again I say unto you that if two of you shall agree on earth as touching anything that you shall ask [within the will of God], it shall be done for you of my Father which is in Heaven.*

This is why James 5:16 ^{AMP} encourages us to *confess our struggles and faults to one another and pray for one another, that we may be healed and restored to a spiritual tone of mind and heart* because *the earnest, heartfelt, and continued prayer of a righteous man makes tremendous power available [dynamic in its working]*. The ^{NLT} says *the earnest prayer of a righteous person has great power and produces wonderful results.* Some Old Testament Scriptures even say *one will put one thousand* (enemies) *to flight, but two will put ten thousand to flight* (Leviticus 26:8; Deuteronomy 32:30, Joshua 23:10). Do we have that many enemies? Yes. Possibly. Remember that satan took one-third of the heavenly hosts with him in his fall.

When we prayed the salvation prayer, we became children of God (Romans 8:15), and just as any loving father wants for his children, Father God wants us to have the relationships and partnerships we need to support and help us in the struggles and trials of life. Psalm 68:6 promises that *God sets the lonely and solitary into families*, and Proverbs 18:24 [AMP] says that we can have loving and reliable friends *who stick closer to us than a brother*.

Make Changes Based on Your Heart's Leading

Learning to yield to the Holy Spirit is another thing that has helped me to be a more positive, balanced, and well-adjusted person, better able to handle the everyday. I work to let the Holy Spirit direct me in even the small details of my life, not as a master lording over me, but as a dear Friend Who has my best interests at heart and Who can see the big picture of things past, present, and future—specific details about my life and the lives of those near me. Psalm 37:23 ^{AMP} says that *the steps of a good man are directed (ordered, established) by the Lord, and He delights in his way and blesses his path*. The Spirit knows whether it's okay for me to participate in various activities, projects, etc., what foods I should eat, and what choices are best to make. His leading isn't to restrict me from having fun or punish me in any way, but to lovingly protect me and make me a more well-rounded person who overall enjoys a life worth living.

Following His direction might lead to changing some things in our lives, but we trust that making those changes will help us in the short-term and in the long run. It takes willingness and faith. We must be willing to lay ourselves bare before God and invite Him to lead us in this way; and in His faithfulness, He will tenderly do so through gentle nudges and promptings, usually felt within our hearts, but not limited to any one form of communication. It could be through a Scripture that speaks to us, a sign or quote we read, an impression we feel, a sermon snippet, a song lyric, the words of a friend or stranger, an article we see, a doctor's advice, a group counseling or individual therapy session, any myriad of ways.

Our enemy satan also tries to **mis**lead us in many of these same ways (2 Corinthians 11:14). To distinguish the leadings of the Spirit, Scripture tells us in James 3:17 that God's wisdom—*the wisdom from above—is pure, peaceable, gentle, loving, compassionate, willing to yield, full of mercy and good fruits, and without partiality or hypocrisy*. It is sincere, wholehearted, and straightforward without being critical, heavy, or condemning. In other words, even when it is corrective, and God has to tell us "how it is" for our own good, it is loving and easily received—not awkward or harsh.

For example, when I got drunk for the first time in years over the ending of a relationship, the next day during my time with God, my Bible practically opened itself to Ephesians 5:18, which says, *be not drunk with wine, which is excess, but be filled with the Spirit.* (That's a slight exaggeration—I actually opened it myself, but the page it opened to and the Scripture that I first saw was no accident!) It was accompanied by such a loving feeling. There was not an ounce of criticism or blame in it. I knew God was saying that getting drunk was not going to help me do anything but temporarily numb myself, but that turning to Him and the Holy Spirit would provide the help I really needed.

The devil, on the other hand, after tempting us with sin, condemns us for succumbing to it. (Isn't that a double whammy?) He wants us to feel unworthy, guilty, and ashamed in order to drive a wedge between us and God. That's what happened to Adam and Eve in the garden. They were used to fellowshipping with God daily until they sinned. Afterward, they felt ashamed and *hid from Him when they heard His voice* (Genesis 3:8). The devil tempted them, and then he condemned them into shame and fear after they succumbed to his temptation. He used condemnation to attempt to separate them from the loving Father who had created them in His own image and placed them in a garden paradise filled with only good.

That's the difference between the Holy Spirit and satan, between conviction and condemnation. God never condemns us and desires only to help us and have a deep and loving companionship with us. Submitting to His corrective conviction *yields His peace and righteousness* (Hebrews 12:11). He doesn't want anything, including sin, separating us from Him. Proverbs 3:12 says *the Lord disciplines those He loves, as a father the son in whom he delights.* But satan is an *enemy to righteousness* (Acts 13:10) and plots against God's saving purposes through his false conviction, which is condemnation. We mustn't fall for it or allow him to pervert God's true ways of interacting with us.

One of the positive changes the Holy Spirit led me into was leaving my abusive marriage. He showed me very plainly in His Word and through His promptings that it was never going to improve and that I could accept deliverance from it instead of being tortured in it (Hebrews 11:35). He shared with me that some women have successfully stood for their spouses and seen them born again and experienced restoration and redemption within their marriages, but that my situation would not have that result or ever change. So it was up to me to make the essential changes that I needed, and I had solid biblical grounds for divorce. It was not an easy or fast process, but His grace was there to help me every step of the way.

In fact, whenever God asks us to do something, He abundantly supplies His grace to help us achieve it. God's grace is a supernatural empowering to accomplish what we need to accomplish—spiritually, physically, mentally, and emotionally—in our everyday lives. (I emphasize, it is NOT just for spiritual endeavors.)

I used to teach grace to my 3-5-year-old Sunday School students like this: I would give them one of those huge plastic bats to swing at a whiffle ball being pitched to them. Of course, the bat was bulky for their little hands and arms, and they would wobble through a swing, usually missing and not able to make contact with the ball. Or the contact would be minimal, and the ball would not go very far. Then after a few attempts like this, I would come behind them, holding the bat with them to steady their swings so that they were able to make full contact with the ball and hit it pretty far. They could easily see that I was helping them to get a better result, and I would explain that God helps us in much the same way that I helped them. Whatever we are attempting, through His grace, He puts His super on top of our natural so that we have supernatural assistance and support with it to be successful.

When we have His grace, victory is guaranteed. Victory may not come easily or quickly, but the level of difficulty we are experiencing will be matched with an equal, enduring, and even surpassing amount of grace! Philippians 4:13 ^{AMP} promises that we have *strength for all things in Christ Who empowers us [ready for anything and equal to anything through Him Who infuses inner strength into us; self-sufficient in Christ's sufficiency]*. Ephesians 4:7 reassures us that each person has been given grace from God, and 2 Corinthians 12:9 ^{MSG} promises that God's grace is all we need because *God's strength comes into its own in our weakness*. In other words, God's power works to help us and is *more than enough, always available regardless of the situation, and shows itself most effectively in our weakness* ^(AMP). Hebrews 4:16 promises that we can *come boldly and with confidence to God's throne of grace to find mercy and grace to help us anytime we need it*!

I literally will not begin a day without asking God for His grace to help me throughout it. I want Him to spend the day with me and to help me to be as successful as possible, whether it is with things that I find challenging and difficult or things that I could otherwise accomplish alone. There are many things that I can do without His help, but why would I when He is so willing to offer it and to graciously provide His supernatural empowerment to coincide with my efforts?

Other changes God has led me into have included leaving stressful jobs, making time for exercise and good nutrition, applying balance and moderation to different areas of my life (foods, drinks, time spent watching TV, etc.), getting an adequate amount of sleep, working hard while also taking time to rest, spending morning time with God before I start my day, removing myself from toxic situations, and choosing friends wisely. All of these things help me to have a more positive self-image and a more balanced perspective on life.

Again, areas that the Holy Spirit may lead us to make changes in may affect our relationships, our employment, our personal habits and practices, our time, whether or not we go to therapy, whether certain medications will help us, the list goes on and on. When we are unsure of which steps to take, James 1:5 assures us that whenever *we lack wisdom* in any area, *we can ask God and He will liberally and generously provide it*. We know and trust that God has our best interests at heart and that He promises to *work all things together for our good* (Romans 8:28) when we give Him permission to direct and lead us in the details of our lives. In fact, James 5:11 [MSG] and Psalm 37:23 [NLT] guarantee us that *He cares right down to the last detail* and *delights in every detail of our lives*.

Forgive

The importance of walking in forgiveness toward others (and forgiving ourselves) cannot be overstated! One major reason for this is because our hearts are the very soil in which we plant God's Word, the nurturing of which is critical to accessing our covenant promises. As that soil, we need to keep our hearts as pure, fertile, and unspoiled as possible, just as we would if we were planting a physical garden. There is no room for bitterness or resentment because they work to choke out the Word essential to our survival, well-being, and success. Forgiveness is so important that Jesus Himself admonishes us in Mark 11:25-26 [AMP] that *when we stand praying, we must forgive anything against anyone so that Father God can forgive us*. Much in the Kingdom of God is reciprocal. He says to *let it drop—leave it—let it go*, from the smallest grudge to the greatest offenses against us. And He cautions that if we don't work toward forgiveness, He cannot forgive us.

But there is much about forgiveness that should be clarified. Even in looking up the word forgive, there is confusion within the dictionary. A solid definition for it is *to cease to feel resentment against (an offender)*. But some of the definitions and synonyms for it are the very reason we struggle with it: *to give up resentment of or claim to requital; to grant relief from payment of; condone, discount, excuse, gloss over, whitewash, ignore*.

When someone has committed a grave offense against us, the last thing we want is for our forgiveness of it to imply that we are condoning it, whitewashing it, or excusing it in some way. We have been wronged! We want them to be sorry for what they've done and have to serve or pay some kind of restitution for it. Isn't this the way our society is set up? Isn't this why our courts are filled with civil and criminal court cases? This idea of needing to right wrongs and be paid for punitive damages, pain, and suffering is valid, isn't it? Of course! It is often unacceptable for us to expect anything less. What would our society be like if we just ignored infractions? Violations would become even more rampant than they currently are.

Even God holds us accountable for wrongs. Isn't this the whole concept behind Heaven, hell, and the need for salvation? But God also asks us *to forgive others as He has forgiven us* (Mark 11:25), and He asks us to *bless those who curse us and pray for those who mistreat us* (Matthew 5:44, Luke 6:28). What is He thinking? Why does He ask us to do something that seems so difficult?

His logic behind it is really rather brilliant! We trust in Isaiah 55:8-9 which tells us that *His thoughts are not our thoughts and His ways are higher than our ways.* In other words, He has a higher perspective than we have, a clearer vision and vantage point than we can see, and He doesn't think the way we think. In fact, our goal is to think **like Him** and have the *mind of Christ* (1 Corinthians 2:16)—to let Him establish our thoughts in His wisdom (Proverbs 16:3 ^{AMPC}). God assures us that He Himself is also concerned about retribution when He emphatically says in Romans 12:19, *vengeance is Mine, and I will repay (requite, take care of it)*! In Deuteronomy 32:35 ^{MSG}, He declares to us that He is *in charge of vengeance and payback*, and that their time is coming. But He also says that He will *show mercy and lovingkindness on whom He chooses* (Exodus 33:19, Romans 9:15-16) and that the sacrifice of Jesus has paid the price for all sin (Ephesians 1:7, Romans 3:24-25, John 1:29) to whomever elects to appropriate His salvation in their lives. If we put the people who hurt us into God's hands, He can take over and decide how to deal with them.

Do you see what this does? It **frees** us to walk without that burden, without that offense weighing us down. It frees us to be emotionally healed, trusting that He is handling it in His infinite wisdom. It works to reestablish peace, grace, wholeness, and rest within our lives, and possibly at some point, within the lives of those who have wounded us. What a relief!

He understands that when we are offended and hurt, the pain can be uncomfortable and sometimes even unbearable. He knows that carrying around emotional scars can hinder us in so many ways and that the sooner we can be rid of offense, the better off we are. He knows holding grudges can lead to high levels of stress and even affect our physical bodies, our health, and well-being. He also knows that sometimes the person who caused our pain will take responsibility and apologize, but that very often, the person who hurt us may never do that for us. Waiting for them to express regret or ask for forgiveness would just extend our pain and grief.

In asking us to forgive them and pray for them, He is releasing **us** from the consequence of **their** choices, from the pain of holding resentment against someone, because resentment eats at our hearts and souls and hinders us from progressing past the hurt. It may seem like forgiveness sometimes imprudently sets them free, but **we** are the ones set free within it. They may or may not ever be free from the consequence of what they did to us (by appropriating the sacrifice Jesus made on man's behalf), but we **can** be free of it. When we work at forgiving them and we pray for them, we are opening the door for God's blessing and love to flow unobstructed within and through our lives—through our hearts, minds, and bodies—healing and restoring us. We are letting God's perfect love settle us and reach every part of us to rectify and reinstate **our** well-being. And who knows whether our prayers for them might actually make a difference in their lives at some point? (Wouldn't that be a kick in satan's teeth since he is our real enemy?)

What forgiveness does **not** do is condone their behavior or excuse their wrongdoing against us. Wrong is still wrong. It doesn't mean we become a doormat and allow people to repeatedly hurt us. God may even prompt us to take some sort of action along with our efforts to pray for them. He may lead us to set firm boundaries for ourselves that protect us from being hurt in the same way again. Applying forgiveness and working through challenges could result in a stronger relationship and bond than was previously had, but that's not always the case—it may mean leaving a relationship or friendship. As in all other things, being led by the Holy Spirit is key to finding the right solutions to the offenses in our lives. Even when we must take Spirit-led action, it is essential that we work to achieve forgiveness while doing so.

For example, when I was attacked, I absolutely wanted to prosecute because I did not want him to have the opportunity to do to anyone else what he did to me. God showed His support to me with His grace to endure the trial, the quick guilty verdict and sentence imposed, and His faithfulness to speak audibly to me to reassure me that He was there. In my divorce, it was necessary to go through court proceedings since it was not amiable. As a single mother, I needed to secure my home and car to help me raise my son. But in the job I recently left, it had come to a point of harassment that was possibly actionable, but I did not feel led to pursue action against them—just to walk in love as well as I could while quietly leaving. In each situation, though, forgiving them and praying for them has helped me to heal, just as I shared above.

Forgiveness is a choice and often a process. It is **not** a feeling. We make the choice by faith. Sometimes we immediately feel better, and sometimes it doesn't make us feel any different at first. Often, I essentially confess my way into it. I pray a prayer very similar to this:

> Father, according to Your Word, I choose to forgive this person for _____. If I have a part that I need to acknowledge within this situation, please show me and help me to fix it. I thank You for leading me in actions that help me to heal and that please You. I ask You to show me how to pray for them. I ask you to bless them, Father, according to Your Word, in Jesus' Name, Amen.

And if the resentment comes back, I restate that I have chosen to forgive them, and I thank God for His grace to walk it out. It gets gradually easier, until one day I realize the pain is greatly lessened or even gone.

Praying for people who have hurt us can lead to some interesting deeds, but we can be assured that God would never lead us in an action that could result in danger to us! If we've been put at risk by someone, God would never direct us to reenter that situation. When I prayed for the man who attacked me, God did not expect or ask me to meet him in any way. But God did lead me to donate to a prison ministry in his behalf and pray for his salvation.

In contrast, God put it on my heart to help my ex-husband get to my son's basketball games and other sports events for a season when he was without transportation, but at no time did I feel the threat of any physical danger in carrying this out. Otherwise, I am positive God would not have led me to provide rides for him.

In other circumstances, I've given gifts that were on my heart, bought treats to leave coworkers who'd slighted me, made lunches and dinners for people who have hurt me, given to various ministries in their behalf, anything I feel safely prompted to do to get me walking in love and past the offenses.

This process is all part of God's genius design to propel us unhindered into the fantastic plans He has for us. *For I know the thoughts and plans I have for you, says the Lord, thoughts and plans for welfare and peace and not for evil, to give you hope in your final outcome* (Jeremiah 29:11). Psalm 139 even tells us He has a *book in which He wrote every good plan He desired for us before we were born* (verse 16), and that His thoughts toward us *outnumber the sand on the seashore* (verse 18). Being committed to forgiveness helps Him establish His plans in our lives.

Give God's Word Opportunity in the Every Day

Joshua 1:8 promises that if we *keep this Book of the Law always on our lips and we meditate on it day and night, so that we are careful to do everything written in it, then we will be prosperous and successful.* Deuteronomy 11:18 encourages us to wholeheartedly impress God's Word on our hearts and souls as if *binding them as signs and reminders on our hands or frontlets between our eyes.* He intends for what we say, see, and do to filter through His Word and reflect His ways because He knows how to make our lives fruitful and abundant. Proverbs 1:9, 3:3, 4:9, 6:21, and many other Scriptures motivate us to internalize God's Word, as we mentioned before, so that it can guide us. Verse 22 of Proverbs 6 even promises that *when we walk about, wisdom will guide us; when we sleep, it will watch over us; and when we awake, it will talk to us.*

But how do we apply this infilling—this need to stay Scriptured-up—to the everyday in the midst of our busy, often hectic lives? I mentioned my vision board earlier, where I wrote down specific Scriptures to study, meditate, and confess, along with pictures of myself as a bride. This was an invaluable tool for that season of my life, and I sometimes still pull it out to remind myself.

I've heard testimonies of people finding it helpful to put specific Scriptures on their bathroom or bedroom mirrors, on their refrigerators, or other places they will see them often to keep them before their eyes and help them stay mindful of them. Listening to sermons on tape or CD during commutes is another way to keep the Word fresh within us. The Word of God, in all of its various forms (Bible, CD, tape, inspirational articles, devotionals, jewelry, framed Scripture prints, handwritten post-it notes, etc.) is food and sustenance for our spirits just as natural food is for our physical man (Job 23:12, Deuteronomy 8:3, Matthew 4:4, Ezekiel 3:3).

Another thing that has been very helpful for me is to record Scriptures that apply to various situations I'm facing, just as I shared earlier in conjunction with my vision board. I still do this! I search out Scriptures that match situations, as we said we'd do when planning or designing our garden—if we need potassium, we plant beets. I take those Scriptures and record them to put on my phone so I can listen to them at night while I sleep, in the mornings while getting ready for the day, on walks, and other times when it is convenient. Sometimes my recordings are pieces of sermons which have hit my heart, but mostly they are Bible passages—covenant promises—recorded in my own voice. This can be very powerful as we tend to believe ourselves more than other voices we hear. There is something very persuasive in hearing God's Word in our own vocal sound. And as I go through the day, this Word that I've planted in my heart pops up here and there from my spirit to speak to me, comfort me, guide me, and give me wisdom, just as Proverbs 6:22 promises.

I also spend about half an hour each morning reading my devotionals and praying before I start my day. This means that I have to set my alarm and plan ahead of time accordingly, and if I oversleep, I have to shuffle around and prioritize my morning to fit it in where I can. My day always, without fail, goes so much better when I start it with God, even if it means I skipped a day washing my hair or made some other adjustment to make time for God.

With some thought and effort, we can find ways to give God's Word the priority it warrants in order to help us, knowing this investment benefits every area of our lives. We can do this while still balancing family, work, our responsibilities, and fun in the mix. In fact, we are most well-balanced when we put God first.

Give Yourself Away to Get Out of Yourself

When life is a struggle and situations, circumstances, and emotions are weighing us down, we must resist letting those problems make us feel overwhelmed. Problems can become the center of our thoughts unless we purposefully redirect our focus and effort in the ways we've described throughout Section Two of this book. When we are in a crisis, we need to magnify our God instead of magnifying our problems or allowing the problems to magnify themselves. We cannot let problems loom larger than God. When we do, it just sets us up for exhaustion, worry, and doubt, which counteract our faith.

Remember that Jesus said He has left us His peace, and we must *not allow or permit ourselves to be fearful, intimidated, or otherwise disturbed* (John 14:27 AMPC). We have to be proactive. Hebrews 4:11 tells us to *labor to enter into His rest*. In other words, put diligent effort forth to rest in our faith—we've renewed our minds, we've prayed, we've planted the seed of God's Word through meditation and confession, we've praised, we've been obedient to the promptings of the Spirit—we're doing everything we know to do, so now we must **rest** in all of that. We must trust the process and the God of the process. When we're doing our part, God will be faithful to His part!

In combination with all of these, another very beneficial strategy is to find a way to help someone else. When I'm helping someone else, it's impossible to stay focused on my problems. It's a way to get my mind off of them and give God time to work.

Philippians 2:4 AMP, MSG tells us to *not only be concerned with ourselves but to also look out for the interests of others, to lend a helping hand*. Proverbs 18:16 AMP says that *a man's gift given in love or courtesy makes room for him*, and God promises that *when we give, it is given to us in return, in good measure and running over* (Luke 6:38).

Our gifts can be in the form of time, talent, possessions, or any way we feel led to contribute. Maybe it's taking a dinner plate to a neighbor, volunteering at a school or nursing home, tutoring a student, working in a soup kitchen, helping someone with housekeeping duties for a season, mowing a yard, shopping for a child from the angel tree, using our design talents to make a flyer or newsletter, giving useful things we no longer need to a mission or Good Will.

We want to follow the promptings within our hearts when giving so that we don't end up saying yes to every worthy venture we find and overcommitting ourselves or losing our balance in other areas of our lives. But when we find ways to bless others, we are allowing God to work on our problems without being overly focused on them, and then suddenly, they don't seem as large and intimidating as they did before. Plus, God promises that what we've *done unto the least of these, we've done unto Him* (Matthew 25:40). It's a win-win for everyone!

Fasting

Fasting should only be undertaken if you feel prompted to do so and should never take precedence over your physical health or a doctor's advice. Also, if you're feeling especially overwhelmed or suicidal right now, it's probably not best to attempt fasting. It may add stress to your efforts to make progress in other more crucial and timely areas. Whenever I have fasted, if I did not feel like I had the grace to continue, I ended the fast immediately. There is no condemnation from God for not completing a fast (Romans 8:1). If a fast is not working properly, quitting is wisdom.

With that said, if you've been applying the principles outlined beforehand in this book successfully and are experiencing progress in your faith, fasting is a great way to receive clarity and grow spiritually within your struggles.

There are many instances within the Bible when our biblical examples undertook personal fasting or declared a fast among a group of people for reasons both spiritual and practical to help them within their immediate circumstances. Moses received the Ten Commandments after a personal fast (Exodus 34:28, Deuteronomy 9:18). Jehoshaphat proclaimed a fast throughout his kingdom to seek God's help in battle (2 Chronicles 20:3). Ezra sought God's protection for a safe journey for his household on their way to Jerusalem through fasting (Ezra 8:21-23). Esther decreed a fast for all the Jews in Susa before she approached the king to ask him to spare the lives of her people which resulted in God delivering the Jews from destruction (Esther 4:16).

There are many types and durations of fasting. Fasting is giving up or abstaining from food, drink, or something else for a period of time to give more attention and focus to God. Some people abstain from food and drink, some fast only on water, some fast food but not liquids, some fast on fruits and/or vegetables only, some fast activities such as social media or television. Similarly, Lent is a type of fasting where people choose one item to give up, such as sugar or chocolate, in the weeks preceding Easter.

I have fasted for as little as twenty-four hours to as long as forty days, often for three-day or twenty-one-day periods. I have never completely abstained from drinks but have refrained entirely from food and have gone on fruit/vegetable fasts. Daniel was on a twenty-one-day fruit and vegetable fast when he was visited by the angel and received the revelation and clarity he sought (Daniel 10:2-14)!

To fast successfully, determine your goal for fasting. Isaiah 58:6-8 tells us that fasting can be a powerful tool for breaking free from many types of difficulty, bondage, and oppression. We must also pray for God's grace to fast and to stop fasting. Remember that God's grace puts His super upon our natural for supernatural results. I remember a time when I was on day thirty of a forty-day fast, push mowing my acre yard with as much stamina as if I hadn't missed a meal. I felt so tuned in to the spiritual realm I almost expected to see an angel pop up at any time. It wouldn't have surprised me in the least! They are always around us in the spirit realm, but we just can't see them with our natural eyes, unless they are instructed to reveal themselves to us.

Confess your grace and God's Word regarding fasting, as well as any Scriptures you are standing on related to your reason for fasting. Job said, and it can be our perspective also, that he *esteemed and treasured the words of His mouth more than his necessary food* (Job 23:12 [AMP]). Moses reminds us that *man does not live by bread only, but by every word which proceeds out of the mouth of the Lord* (Deuteronomy 8:3). Jesus repeated it for us in His reply to satan while He was being tempted in the wilderness when He said, "*It has been written, man shall not live and be upheld and sustained by bread alone, but by every word which comes forth from the mouth of God* (Matthew 4:4 [AMPC], Luke 4:4 [AMPC])."

During a fast, especially during extended times of fasting, it is crucial that we take time to feed ourselves spiritually with God's Word. The

Scripture we feed our spirit man is replacing the food our natural man is used to receiving to operate the various functions within our bodies. Proverbs 4:20, 22 ^{NKJV} says *my son, give attention to my words; incline your ear to my sayings. For they are life to those who find them, and health to all their flesh.* Psalm 119:103 ^{NAS} says *how sweet are Your words to my taste! Yes, sweeter than honey to my mouth!* Ezekiel 3:1-2 ^{MSG} also compares God's Word to spiritual food when it says *He told me, "Son of man, eat what you see. Eat this book. Then go and speak to the family of Israel. Make a full meal of it!" So, I ate it. It tasted so good—just like honey!*

It is also very important during fasting that we guard our hearts and our time. The times when fasting has been difficult for me have been the times when I let myself run down and didn't take the time to stay in a place of grace. I chose activities which drained me when I needed to stay plugged in for the duration of my fasting. This can happen easily if we overcommit ourselves during this time. If this happens—if we find ourselves suddenly in a tough spot during fasting—we must get back into our place of grace quickly! Pray, maybe ask a covenant friend to add his or her prayers also, and step back into our grace. (It may also mean ending the fast if we feel like we should.)

Fasting can be a very powerful spiritual tool, and it is one of my favorite things! The grace for fasting is so tangible, and it always reminds me how that same grace which keeps my body going during a fast just as if I were eating is also the grace we have for every other area of our lives, for God's promises of healing, finances, family salvation, and general day to day things. It yields immediate and obvious benefits as well as profiting us in less obvious ways that intertwine with other areas of our lives.

Tithing

Tithing is a scriptural and spiritual principle which can positively impact our lives, but like fasting, if you are feeling overwhelmed with battling suicidal thoughts and just getting through the day, you may want to save this until you're in a better place. Money can be a stressful issue that adds to the pressure we feel in other areas of our lives, and tithing (or not tithing) isn't intended to be something that causes us to come under condemnation, but rather to enhance our covenant blessings.

This being said, tithing is another way to give of ourselves practically and metaphorically and show that we honor and trust God. Practically, there are several biblical promises concerning tithing that we line ourselves up to receive when we tithe. Metaphorically, our jobs and the income from them are such a big part of who we are and how we spend large portions of our time that honoring God with a percentage of the increase from them demonstrates a higher level of faith toward Him.

Tithing means to give ten percent of our increase to the Lord. Deuteronomy 14:22 tells us to *be sure to set aside a tenth of all that our fields produce each year*. Proverbs 3:9 says that we should *honor the Lord with our possessions, and with the first fruits of all our increase*. Verse 10 says when we honor God in this way, *our barns will be filled with plenty*. When asked whether we should be subject to paying taxes, Jesus answered that we should *render therefore unto Caesar the things which are Caesar's; and unto God the things which are God's* (Matthew 22:21). We can certainly apply His statement about the things which are God's to tithing.

Jesus also said we should not *lay up for ourselves treasures on earth, where moth and rust destroy and where thieves break in and steal; but we should lay up for ourselves treasures in Heaven, where neither moth nor rust destroys and where thieves do not break in and steal. For where our treasure is, there our hearts will be also* (Matthew 6:19-21). The

^AMP^ says *for where your treasure is, there your heart [your wishes, your desires, that on which your life centers] will be also*. The ^MSG^ asks, *it's obvious, isn't it? The place where your treasure is, is the place you will most want to be, and end up being.* This goes with what we discussed earlier about setting our hearts, minds, and affections on heavenly things.

From Jesus's teaching above, I've always thought of the tithe as a way to circumcise or consecrate and make holy our hearts and our finances from the stress money can bring. His teaching here doesn't mean that we shouldn't have ample or even abundant finances or that it's wrong to be blessed financially. This would be illogical since the covenant God made with Abraham resulted in him being extremely wealthy, and Job was restored double by God Himself on the other side of his struggles (Genesis 13:2, Job 42:10). There are many Scriptures which prove that *the blessing of the Lord makes rich, and He adds no sorrow to it* (Proverbs 10:22). Biblical saints were often the most blessed people around (King David, King Solomon, Abraham, Isaac, Jacob, etc.).

The key is to be good stewards with money while putting our faith and trust in God, where they rightly belong. Tithing isn't a benefit for God or the Church; it's to help us! As the saying goes, "Money makes an excellent servant but a lousy master," so by being willing to consecrate it through the tithe, I am helping to make sure I keep its importance in proper perspective. First Timothy 6:10 admonishes that *the **love** of money is the root of all sorts of evil*, **not** money itself. Remember Jesus said in John 10:10 that it is *the thief* who *comes to steal, kill, and destroy*, but He came to *give us life, to the full, until it overflows*. Second Corinthians 9:8 adds that God wants us to *always have all sufficiency in all things and abundance for every good deed*.

The act of tithing aligns us with covenant privileges specific to finances, possessions, and spiritual things. For example, God says if we will *bring our tithes into the storehouse* (symbolic for His Church, His endeavors), we can *prove Him now herewith to open for us the windows of Heaven, and pour out for us a blessing, that there shall not be room enough to receive it.*

And He promises to *rebuke the devourer* (satan) *for our sakes, so he shall not destroy the fruits of our ground; neither shall our vine cast her fruit before the time in the field, saith the LORD of hosts* (Malachi 3:10-12). This rebuke He projects to satan on our behalf prevents him from devouring our finances, our possessions, our spiritual gardens, our families, etc. Something I read recently said that giving God His ten percent protects the other ninety percent for us! It said **give God what is His, and He will protect what is yours**. Our money and possessions will go further and last longer than they otherwise would, and when satan tries to destroy things, we can claim tither's rights with our faith to walk in this protection and restoration.

These *windows*, this *field*, this *fruit*, this *harvest* certainly also represents the harvest of God's Word that we've learned to plant within the pages of this book to bring about positive changes in our lives and to help us overcome the struggles we are facing.

When I'm doing everything I know to do to be blessed, to stay healthy spirit, soul, and body, to avoid wrong thinking, and to walk in relationship with God, tithing gives me a way to put my money where my mouth is (to borrow that expression) and add another, deeper layer to my covenant promises. If I'm speaking the Word, wearing my armor, planting and tending my garden, weeding out wrong or disabling thoughts, applying spiritual principles and truths to guarantee success and bless my life so that I can effectively battle the temptation to quit or give up, then I take comfort in and rejoice that I have the opportunity to tithe and further empower all those efforts. Instead of being concerned that I can't afford to do it, it becomes obvious that I can't afford **not** to.

Although tithing is another way to connect with God and His covenant at a greater level, it is not meant to add stress or to be a difficult rule that we must follow, heavy or condemning in any way. Second Corinthians 9:7 ᴬᴹᴾ tells us to *let each one of us give [thoughtfully and with purpose] just as he has decided in his heart, not grudgingly or under compulsion, for God loves a cheerful giver [and delights in the one whose heart is in his gift].*

There have been many times when I've tithed consistently, and even written and dropped a $30,000 check into the offering without batting an eye or thinking twice about it (that's a lot of money for a girl who grew up in extreme poverty), and times when I have worried about and kept from giving small fractions of that amount.

In a sense, tithing, for me, can be a heart-gauge of sorts because it reminds me to keep my confidence in God since I can't out-give Him and He is always faithful to give back to me, *good-measure, pressed-down, shaken together, and running over* (Luke 6:38). If I'm hesitating to tithe, I am needing to reexamine and calibrate the condition of my heart and thoughts. I do not want to tie God's hands from being able to bless me as abundantly as He wants by not trusting Him enough to tithe when He is my greatest Ally and has such good intentions and plans for me.

To summarize, the benefits of tithing are:

- God giving back to us financially and spiritually in much greater measure (much like Jesus multiplying the fish and loaves of the small boy who cheerfully gave (Luke 9:16, John 6:11))

- the windows of Heaven open over us (windows allow us to be able to see with a heavenly perspective and godly wisdom, as well as being able to receive through an open window or door)

- giving us a concise way to circumcise our hearts and our finances so that they are holy and consecrated to God

- allowing God to rebuke the devourer (satan) for our sakes to accompany and further empower all of the steps we are taking to overcome and defeat him.

As in all things, we should be willing to take this idea of tithing before God in prayer and let the Holy Spirit lead us in how we respond to His direction. The good news is that when we do this, we can't really miss Him! He will reveal to us in His loving way what He expects and if, when, and where to give. He may put it on our hearts to tithe or to wait while we focus on more critical areas. Either way, we will be additionally strengthened and empowered as a result of our willingness to be led by Him.

What if It Seems Like It's Not Working?

There have been many times in my life when I prayed about something I needed God to fix, and I saw almost immediate results. Little things and big things. Life-changing things and every day, ordinary things. There were times I needed books for classes and didn't have the money, but then something would work out almost immediately to cover them. Everything from open parking spaces I asked God to provide because I didn't want to walk across campus in stormy weather to court appearances as part of my divorce proceedings.

For example, I once had to defend myself in court when my ex-husband surprised me by filing a last-minute order to attempt to make me responsible for his legal fees. I had very little time to prepare or money to hire an attorney. I got on my face before God and asked Him to help me represent myself. Then I prayerfully went through my massive four-year collection of court documents and pulled out everything I felt the slightest inkling to take to court with me. It was miraculous! For every point his attorney tried to present as a reason I should have to pay, I had a document with me to use in rebuttal against it. In spite of the attorney's vehement objections, the judge dismissed the claim almost immediately in my favor.

And there have been times when I had to stand for quite a while before I saw the results I'd prayed for. For instance, during an extremely stressful time before my divorce, I got a ticket for speeding that left me very discouraged and disheartened. I was driving home from my parents on a road I had traveled every weekday for several years on my daily commute, and I'd never noticed an awkwardly placed speed limit sign at the bottom of a steep hill where the speed abruptly went from 55 mph to 35 mph. I actually had been speeding because I thought the speed zone started at the **second** 35 mph sign. When I prayed about it, I felt led to plant and speak the Scripture in Colossians 2:14 [AMPC] which says *Christ has cancelled, blotted out, and wiped away the handwriting of the note (bond) with its legal decrees and demands which was in force and stood against us (hostile to us); this [note with its regulations,* *decrees, and demands] He set aside and cleared completely out of our way by nailing it to [His] cross.*

The part about the *bond with its legal decrees* sounded like it would cover a ticket to me, with a very strong promise attached to remove it completely. So I planted that Scripture as a promise for it, and called it, "Dismissed!" And I began to put some action toward doing my part to make it happen. I met with the pre-court secretary. She referred me to the officer who wrote the ticket. He referred me to the prosecutor who would be in court that day. The prosecutor said he was unable to help me. But at each juncture, I kept thanking God it was dismissed regardless of how it looked (looking not at the things which were seen (them not helping me) and holding on to the unseen (God's promise to cancel it)(2 Corinthians 4:18)).

I had gone through every person whom I was told may help me to no avail, and I had prayed and believed for weeks before the court date that God would dismiss it. In the end, He did just that. We got right up to the judge, me still saying under my breath, "Thank you God for dismissing this!" The judge asked whether I would plead guilty or not guilty, and I replied, "Your honor, I was technically guilty because I didn't realize that is where the speed zone began." I was attempting to explain where it happened and how I thought the second sign was the beginning of the speed zone, and before I even got that much out, he exclaimed, "Oh...I know where this sign is! I've never agreed with that speed limit there! I am dismissing this!" And then it was over. My weeks of planting and weeding, confessing, and thanking God manifest triumphantly in a few short minutes before the judge. It looked like nothing was happening until the moment when it really counted, and then God's Word yielded the harvest I'd sown it to accomplish.

But there have also been some extremely painful and confusing times when things did not turn out the way I prayed. Times when I did not understand where God was in my circumstances or what the delay or miscommunication was in the way things were going. Let me share a few of those experiences because they happen to everyone, and the resulting discouragement can be very intense.

I met my ex-husband a little over a year after he had been in an almost-fatal accident. The night he wrecked, he was very intoxicated and under the influence of drugs when he drove his car into a construction dumpster sitting beside the road and extending a couple of feet into the street. Because it did not have proper safety markings around it, he sued the company, and shortly after our son was born, he received a confidential settlement amount that we used to purchase our home and an apartment triplex, as well as other things like vehicles and furniture.

When the company had met with him prior to our relationship, the most they had offered him in settlement was $10,000 because they intended to show he was negligently at fault with his blood alcohol levels and the drugs he had within his system, and they intended to put his friends he'd spent the evening with on the stand to testify about the night in question. They only offered him that small amount because they figured they'd spend that much anyway in legal fees and court costs. But at the admission of both sides (their attorney and ours), the chance of a jury finding negligence on the part of the company became more plausible when he now had a wife and infant to sit next to him in court. So on the one hand, the money he had was non-marital according to previous precedents and the fact that I didn't know him at the time of his wreck, but on the other hand, he most likely would not have been awarded the amount he received if he hadn't had our help to make a jury look at him in a more compassionate light than they would have otherwise seen him.

When the long-awaited result of our divorce proceedings was declared, the judge awarded him—even after his abusive behaviors, infidelity, and recurring drug use—ownership of practically everything the two of us shared. I was only awarded my car (which he had fought to keep) and given the option of living in my home until our son turned eighteen years old, if I paid the monthly mortgage and moved out afterward. It was just about the worst way this situation could have gone!

I was, however, awarded sole custody of our son. He was only granted visitations. It was as if the judge was saying, this court doesn't believe he is capable of raising your child—we don't trust him with a child—we see how he is—but we have to follow the precedent set in these types of cases where things can be classified as non-marital assets.

At the same time that I was receiving this outcome, midpoint two years into my divorce proceedings, I believed that God had been showing me during my prayer time a potential relationship with a godly man from my church. I tried to be very careful to just put it on the back burner and see what happened. I confidentially asked for godly counsel from my spiritual leaders about how to proceed. I told God if it was Him showing me these things, He'd be the one bringing it about because I was simply waiting to see if it came to pass. But because I had entrusted these heart-thoughts to some of my closest friends there, it was becoming a huge rumor that was about to blow up in my face. He married someone else, and it looked as if I had been at fault when that was never my intention at all.

In addition, the person who was in prison for raping and sodomizing me had enlisted the help of an innocence project to attempt to get out. They did more advanced DNA testing than was available thirteen years prior on some of the evidence from the rape kit. But the evidence they successfully tested was from consensual sex I had during one of the promiscuous times I mentioned earlier. It happened several days before the attack occurred and outside of the time frame I had been asked about in court, so I did not offer up the information because, as I previously mentioned, I felt I was already on trial in the eyes of the jury and courtroom attendees. The person I had been with was of mixed race, and based on those DNA results, the man who attacked me was released from prison (owing more time for infractions during his incarceration than he had served) and hailed as a victim of the system.

What they were not able to test any further was some of the other DNA they had collected, making such statements as the results were inconclusive and could not definitively include or exclude him as a source of the DNA which was present, and they seemed to ignore that there was evidence of hair follicles from him that had already shown him being the culprit within 1:152 individuals matching that mitochondrial DNA sequence. They also did not review that just a couple of days after the incident, he had pawned something which had been stolen a few houses down the street at a neighboring location on the same night of my attack and during the same time frame the attack had occurred, placing him absolutely in proximity to me that night. (We live in a very small town, and there were not 152 individuals who were later arrested for theft in the exact same locality or who completely matched the sketch I had provided after the attack and were picked out in the line-up by me; there was only one.)

The newspapers were abuzz with stories about his impending freedom. There were waves of shame, embarrassment, and fear rushing at my heart and mind. After his release, I not only had to be concerned for my safety, but the safety of my small son. I almost crossed paths with him at Walmart, me trying to quickly leave before being seen by him. I was at dinner with my family sitting at a table that he walked by in a restaurant, my father whispering in my ear to not be afraid because he was there to protect me. I was anxiously wondering how many more times I might accidentally end up near him in our small town—or if he'd look for me because sketchy people were getting word to me that he was watching me.

I also came home one evening from church to find that the water line going into my icemaker had broken, and water was flooding the kitchen floor and gushing down the walls of my basement, through light switches, onto my carpet.

Each of these devastating events (losing my house, the incidents at church, my attacker being released from prison, a broken water line) happened within days of one another—a no holds barred onslaught from the pit of hell landing on me at the same time. (One of satan's most intricate details during this blitz was that the signature on many of the DNA testing documents was the lab-employed Senior father of the Junior son whom I had thought God was speaking to my heart about. I honestly believe in the natural, it was a coincidence—this man did not even know me to have a grudge against me—but in the spirit realm, it was orchestrated by satan to add fuel to the fires with which he was assailing me. I told you satan is almost as intricate in his details for evil against us as God is for our good. Hand overplayed once again!)

Can you imagine where I was emotionally with all of these events collectively coming at me at once? The devil had hit me with his best shots—thrown more than I could ever imagine at me at one time—and I was losing my church family of thirteen years in the fallout. It looked like things could not conceivably be any worse.

What do we do when we are faced with more than we can possibly handle? How do we react when the rug is pulled, jerked, forcibly yanked completely out from under us? When we can't see God, can He still see us? When we can't feel Him, is He still there? When we don't know why things are happening the way they are happening and we don't have the clarity we need, how do we proceed? When it looks easier to give up and give in than to **get** up and **press** in, how do we keep going?

We do what Daniel did when he was thrown into the lion's den (Daniel 6:16). We do what David did when he fought the bear and the giant (1 Samuel 17:36, 50). We do what Abraham did when he left his home to go to the land God told him to search and when he placed his beloved and promised son on the altar ready to follow God's instructions concerning him (Genesis 12:4, 22:9). We do what Shadrach, Meshach, and Abednego did when they were thrown into the fiery furnace (Daniel 3:21). What Esther did when her people were decreed to be murdered (Esther 8:3-6). What Joseph did when he was cast into prison for a crime he didn't commit (Genesis 39:9, 20). What Jesus did when He could no longer feel His Father's presence in the midst of hanging on our cross, and cried out to Him, *My God, My God, Why hast Thou forsaken me* (Matthew 27:46).

We keep on keeping on. We stick with the plan. We continue with the program. We stay in faith. We trust God. We speak the Word. We work the steps in this book. We keep seeking and praying for Wisdom, while putting unanswered questions on the back burner so they don't hinder our progress. We keep internalizing God's Word and building our image from the inside out. We keep wearing our spiritual armor. We keep following our heart's leading. We keep walking in forgiveness to the best of our ability. We keep giving God's Word opportunity every day. We keep giving ourselves away. We fast and tithe our increase when led. We put one foot in front of the other over and over.

And then we do it all again the next day the best that we can, and the day after that, and the day after that. **And eventually things get better.** Gradually, we DO *see the goodness of the Lord in the land of the living* (Psalm 27:13). God is always faithful. He is always with us, even when it feels like we're alone. He **will** rescue us. He **will** deliver us. He **will** comfort us. He **will** reward us. He **will** avenge us. He **will**.

You've probably heard of blind faith. That's what it can feel like when we are walking through very dark and troubled times. **But that's okay because faith doesn't look at what we can see anyway** (2 Corinthians 4:18)! Faith doesn't look at the things we see in the natural realm, but instead at the unseen greater Truth of God's Word and covenant. Faith looks with the *eyes of our heart* (Ephesians 1:18). We know by faith that God's Truth overrules facts! We know our faith can make us whole—Jesus said it to those He healed, "*Your faith has made you whole* (Mark 5:34, 10:52, Luke 7:50, 17:19)."

We are growing even when we can't see it. God is working even when it looks like nothing is happening. *We walk by faith, not by sight* (2

Corinthians 5:7). Again, we *believe to see the goodness of the Lord in the land of the living,* **in this present life** (Psalm 27:13^{GNT}). We trust that God has **good** plans for us just like He said (Jeremiah 29:11)! *His thoughts toward us outnumber the sand* (Psalm 139:17-18).

And if you are in your first experiences of a new faith, and you're thinking, *keep on keeping on? I haven't started yet*, then start now! Go back and reread those last few paragraphs and everywhere you see words like *keep*, plug in the word *start*. We *start* keeping on. We *start* with the plan. We *start* with the program. We *start* in faith. We *start* trusting God. We *start* speaking the Word. We *start* working the steps in this book. We *start* seeking and praying for Wisdom, while putting unanswered questions on the back burner so they don't hinder our progress. We *start* internalizing God's Word and building our image from the inside out. We *start* wearing our spiritual armor. We *start* following our heart's leading. We *start* walking in forgiveness to the best of our ability. We *start* giving God's Word opportunity every day. We *start* giving ourselves away. We *start* fasting and tithing our increase when led. We *start* putting one foot in front of the other over and over. And then we do it all again the next day the best that we can, and the day after that, and the day after that. You get the idea.

So, satan had hit me with everything he could muster at once, and I was wobbling, but by the grace of God, I was still standing. I appealed the court's decision about my house, and I continued to fight for it for two more years until I was its sole owner. As I mentioned, this entire process was four years long and accumulated $10,000 of attorney fees which my attorney graciously settled for half of, but God and I got there together. Now I have a home that is eighty percent paid off and is something I love and can afford as a single mother, with these amazing neighbors who've become an extension of my family over the twenty-five years I've lived here.

And instead of being property-related, the countless court appearances became custody-related for the next decade. I would have to appear to defend myself against petitions he would file that made allegations like 'she don't feed him no food; she don't buy him no clothes' which had been hastily scrawled onto ripped-up scraps of paper and filed against me. God went with me to every court date, and they finally stopped when my son turned eighteen.

In regard to my attack, it became clear to me thirteen years after I audibly heard the Lord speak to me, saying "Don't worry, child. He's guilty!" that not only was He making sure I knew He was with me during the trial **that** day, but He was **looking forward** to the point in time over a decade down the road when many of the people in our community would doubt his guilt and presume his innocence, to reassure me that He **knew** and **foresaw** it even back then. This really excites me! He is the *Alpha and the Omega*, the *Beginning and the End*, and Everything in between (Revelation 22:13). He is not limited to the constraints of time as we are. There is nothing that happens in our lives that catches Him off guard, so the fact that He saw the future and so clearly spoke to me about it years before it happened is very comforting and proves how much He cares, even with all of the unfairness present within everything about that situation. I can only trust that He has a plan for using how things turned out, since He causes all things to work together for our good (Romans 8:28)(even though He's not the cause of all things), and that hopefully He is somehow able to bring healing and salvation from it for everyone involved, including my attacker.

And I am still waiting for my Ephesians 5 relationship whenever God wants to bring it to me, and with whomever He chooses. I call it my Ephesians 5 relationship because I want what verses 25 and 28 of that chapter mention—someone who *loves me as himself* and *loves me the way Christ loves the Church*—but I'm very happy just being with Him in the meantime.

What is our take-away from this? Don't give up when things get tough! Don't stop when they seem to take much longer than they should! Abraham waited for years before his promised son arrived (Hebrews

6:15). David waited for years to be crowned king after God placed that designation on him (1 Samuel 16:13, 2 Samuel 5:3). Joseph endured years of hardships before achieving the promotion God ordained for him which also brought deliverance to everyone in his and surrounding nations (Genesis 50:20).

There are times I still battle suicidal thoughts. (It's possible that this side of Heaven I always will since satan is behind them and remains my enemy.) Sometimes they are subtle, and sometimes they feel like a sucker-punch which leaves me temporarily breathless. Usually, they relate back to one of the triggers I mentioned earlier. When they attack, I keep working the steps in this book. And the steps work their magic once again. They work because of Jesus, my strong Foundation Who ensures their success and supplements my efforts within His eternal covenant (Matthew 7:24-25, Luke 6:48, 1 Corinthians 3:11, Isaiah 28:16).

They will work for you too if you make Him your foundation. And within the hardships a day can bring, there are also countless opportunities to find things to be grateful for. Family and friends to appreciate while we are blessed to be with them. Children to love on before they grow up. Sunrises and sunsets that gift our day with their beauty. Jobs when many are unemployed. Homes and meals when many are without.

A preacher I value often says that life is not just about the destination, but about the journey. We have to enjoy where we are on the way to where we're going. This is very wise advice.

I hope the steps within this book empower you to do just that, and I pray that you are strengthened within your hearts and souls to overcome every negative thought and action which satan sends to you. You are valuable and loved immeasurably by Father God, Jesus, and the Holy Spirit, as well as so many other people in your life! And just like me, you DO have a life worth living. Let's get busy living it **on purpose;** our stories aren't over yet.

Appendix: Scripture Arsenal/Lies Exposed

It is important to have a collection of covenant Scriptures that will speak to your heart and calm your mind. As you find Scriptures which cover the areas you need, meditate them, plant them in the fertile soil of your heart, and speak them during your prayer times to yield the life that is concealed inside them. In times of struggle and battle, use them as your sword of the Spirit to fight satan's lies—they are excellent lie-replacement truths.

Search them out in your favorite translations! Highlight them. Make notes next to them. Let the Bible be your study guide and the Holy Spirit your tutor. Print them out or write them onto post-its. Put them before your eyes! Record them to listen to while you're doing other things to keep them in your ears.

Often, I will look at the same Scripture in many translations because each presents a basic truth with different imageries and interpretations. (Remember how *sozo* means so many different things and can lose much of its value in translation from Greek to English?) Take them and make them your own! Put the pieces of each one that you like together to become your personal blueprint.

For example, below are several interpretations of a Scripture I meditate and confess often when I'm in the midst of hearing those suicidal voices. Each one of these translations speaks to me in different ways.

- *I'm **sure** now I'll see God's goodness in the exuberant earth. Stay with God! Take heart. **Don't quit**. I'll say it again: Stay with God.* (Psalm 27:13-14 MSG)
- *Still I am **certain** to see the goodness of the LORD in the land of the living. Wait patiently for the LORD; be strong and courageous. Wait patiently for the LORD....* (Psalm 27:13-14 BSB)
- *Yet I am confident I will see the LORD's goodness while I am here in the land of the living.* (Psalm 27:13 NLT)

- *I know that **I will live** to see the LORD's goodness **in this present life***. (Psalm 27:13 ^{GNT})

See what I mean? Each version tells me a similar message of hope which comes together to strengthen my resolve, calm my emotions, and dispel fear and discouragement. Technology has made it easier than ever to access Scripture in more versions than we have ever been previously exposed to, and in many different languages. There are some great Bible apps and websites that allow you to go to a Scripture and then push a button or two to compare versions or make parallel translation comparisons without ever needing to purchase anything or pick up a paper book.

Remember the strategy we learned when we need to counteract satan's lie with God's Truth:

- **Recognize the lie**
- **Cast down and reject the lie:** I cast that thought down in Jesus' Name!
- **Replace the lie with Truth**

Following are common lies that satan uses to attempt to deceive us, and the Truth of what God's Word actually says instead. Some of these may be lies that you have heard. This is an appendix of sorts to expose them so that they are powerless within our lives.

Lie: God doesn't care about me. I'm just one of seven billion people on the planet. He probably doesn't even know me.

Truth: Though it can be easy to feel small and unnoticed in such a big world, God has had you and me on His mind since before creation! Ephesians 1:3-6 ^{MSG} assures us that *long before God laid down the foundations of the earth, He had us in mind, had settled on us as the focus of His love, to be made whole and holy by His love. Long, long ago*

He decided to adopt us into His family through Jesus Christ and *what pleasure He took in planning this*!

Do you know that God is such a planner that before we were even born, He had literally planned every day of our lives the way a loving parent wants to plan good things for his child (Psalm 139:16)? And Jeremiah 29:11 lets us confidently know that those planned days contain *thoughts and plans for welfare, peace, and well-being, plans to prosper us, take care of us, and give us the future we hope for*. This Scripture also clarifies that the plans contain *no evil, no plans to abandon us, no disaster, no harm*. So every time we face situations and circumstances which are harmful, we can be confident that it does not in any way, shape, or form, line up to God's will for our lives, and we can replace the lie that God is somehow allowing this or even authoring this situation with the Truth that He **only** has good plans for us and that He **does** love us and hold us dear.

In fact, Psalm 139 tells us that God *knows us intimately* and *understands our thoughts* before we think them, and He even knows *the words we haven't uttered* yet. It also says He lovingly *knit us together in our mothers' wombs*, and His *thoughts toward us are too numerous to count* because *they would be more in number than the sand of the sea*. Thus, the Truth is that God does know each one of us very well and He cares for us deeply. That's why it's so important to get with God's plan for our lives.

Lie: My life will never get any better. I will always be sick, poor, and defeated.

Truth: The only way this will be accurate is if we continue to think this way! There is a common saying that "attitude determines altitude," so let's look at Truth from a scriptural perspective to get us into a better frame of mind. This will allow God to work more effectively on our behalf so that He can get those good plans mentioned above, plans He's had before we were even born, into motion for us. As we keep moving forward in the things of God, keeping His promises in our hearts and at the forefront of our thoughts and actions, and working the steps mentioned within the pages of this book, Proverbs 4:18 promises that our *paths will become brighter and clearer, just like the morning light of dawn shines brighter and brighter until it reaches the full strength and glory of a perfect day.* Perfect days are what God desires for us, just like the Garden of Eden before man's fall. Deuteronomy 11:21 ᴷᴶⱽ tells us we can have *days of Heaven upon earth*!

Lack, sickness, and defeat are under the Curse, elaborately described in Deuteronomy 28:15-68, that came upon the earth in the garden. But Galatians 3:13 promises us that we are *redeemed from the curse and doom of the Law, Christ having been made a curse for us and purchasing our freedom from it* so that we can have the blessings of a sure and certain covenant with God, also richly detailed in Deuteronomy 28, verses 1-14.

Within this covenant, just as with all of the trials Joseph faced, whatever happens to us that is *meant for evil, God turns and works into His good plans for us* (Genesis 50:20). In fact, Romans 8:28 promises that even though God doesn't cause all of the things we encounter, He does *cause all things to work together and fit into a plan for our good.*

Did you know that, not only has God redeemed us from the curses mentioned, but He wants to give us double for our trouble, just like He did for Job (Job 42:10)? Isaiah 61:7 promises that *instead of our former shame, we should expect a double portion,* and *instead of humiliation we will shout for joy over our portion, we will possess a double portion in our land,* and *everlasting joy will be ours*. This is also echoed in Zechariah 9:12 where God assures us that if we hold onto our hope, *this very day He is declaring that He will restore double to us*. Every day is *this very day*—today. This promise renews **every single day**.

So we have every reason to believe, expect, and confidently know that our lives will **not** always be the same, that our **best** days are ahead of us, and that the **best is, indeed, yet to come**.

Lie: I can't live without this person.

Truth: A simple yet profound truth is that many of the relationships we can become involved in are codependent and toxic to us when viewed with a wrong perspective or undertaken in a wrong context.

When we put our hope in another person, especially to the point that we feel we can't survive without him or her, we are setting ourselves up for failure. The only person we can put this much expectation upon is God Himself. It is unfair and self-defeating to put that kind of pressure on anyone else because it is inevitable that people will disappoint us and sometimes be disappointed by us. They may even reject us or end a relationship, whether it's a business partnership, a friendship, or a romantic bond. At that point, the unbalanced hope we've placed within them can leave us feeling completely forsaken. That's why Scripture tells us that *it is better to put our trust in God than in man* (Psalm 118:8).

In Hebrews 13:5 ^{AMPC}, God Himself promises He will *not in any way fail us, nor give us up, nor leave us without support.* He says, *I will not, I will not, I will not in any degree leave you helpless, nor forsake you, nor let you down, nor relax My hold on you! Assuredly not!*

This is a hefty promise worthy of our complete faith, hope, and trust. When the other relationships in our lives balance upon our relationship with Him, they can take on their proper perspectives and contexts.

In addition to a strong relationship with God, we need strong and honest relationships with ourselves. We cannot hinge our self-worth on a relationship with another person because if that person is removed for any reason, we are left severely lacking. It's like trying to build a house on sand. We have to be comfortable with ourselves and realize our worth from who God says we are to be on sure footing for the other relationships within our lives. In Colossians 3:3-4, we see that our *real identities are hidden with Christ in God*, and *as He is revealed* to us through time spent with Him and in studying His Word, *we are revealed also*—we begin to know who we really are! Just a chapter before, in Colossians 2:10, we see that we are *made complete* and *brought to* the healthy, balanced *fullness* we need *through our union with Him*.

It was such a revelation to me when I was struggling with my self-image to learn that it is okay to love myself, to let the Holy Spirit lead me in having balance in my life, and to be diligent about taking care of myself. Sometimes we are taught to put ourselves at the bottom of the totem pole, with the general impression that everyone else is more important than we are. Jesus tells us—commands us actually—in the Gospels (Luke 10:27, Matthew 22:36-40, Mark 12:28-31) to love our neighbors as ourselves. He said it is the second greatest commandment, the first being to love the Lord our God with all our heart, soul, and strength. Again, the **second greatest commandment** is that we love our neighbors **as (or equal to)** ourselves.

Do you see the implications? If we take the old algebra approach where *a=b* so *b=a*, then we can look at it like this: [love for neighbor] = [love for self], and [love for self] = [love for neighbor]. That means God **expects** us to love ourselves, to treat ourselves as we would treat the people we care about within our lives. There is such a regulating balance in this equation. If like me, you haven't loved yourself as you should, we see now that we have God's **permission** to do so. If we've loved ourselves more than we should, we need to find ways to be less about ourselves and more about others.

Either way, strong and stable relationships with both God and ourselves will allow us to be most prepared to be in healthy relationships with other people, without codependency, and with God's leading, timing, and grace.

In regard to romance, God has a design for us. In Ephesians 5:25, 28, 33, Scripture instructs *husbands to love their wives as Christ loves the church* and as they *love their own bodies* (*a=b* again). Verse 33 ^{AMPC} also paints a beautiful picture of how wives should *respect and reverence their husbands (noticing them, honoring them, preferring and esteeming them, deferring to them, praising them, and loving and admiring them exceedingly)*. To accomplish all of that (it's really a tall order to maintain on a consistent basis), we must follow God's leading in making careful choices so that grace, strength, and balance are there.

When our priority, dependency, and expectations are centered upon God, our other relationships are within the right contexts and perspectives, and we realize He is truly the only person we can't live without.

Lie: I've made too many mistakes to start over. I've gone too far in the wrong direction.

Truth: There isn't anywhere we can go that is too far for Jesus to reach us. In Psalm 139:7-8, we see that there is nowhere in the expanse between Heaven and hell or anywhere in between where God's Spirit can't find us, where God's Love can't rescue us. *No darkness too dark; darkness and light are the same to Him* (verse 12). The psalmist said, *if I make my bed in hell, You are even there*. Romans 8:39 assures us there is no *height or depth in all of creation that can separate us from the love of God which is in Christ Jesus our Lord*.

In Ephesians 3:18-19 ^{AMP}, the apostle Paul echoes the expansive and *extravagant dimensions* of God's Love when he prays that *we will be able to know through our own personal experience—to understand and comprehend—this amazing and endless Love with its breadth and length and height and depth* that allows Christ to reach us anywhere we are.

We simply can't be too far away from God for Him to reach us. The psalmist says in Psalm 40:2 [AMP] that *he was drawn up by the Lord out of a horrible pit of tumult and destruction, out of miry clay, froth, and slime, and his feet were set upon a rock to steady his steps and establish his goings.* James 4:8 tells us that if we *draw near to God, He will draw near to us.* If we *come close to God, He will come close to us* [NLT]. It only takes our decision to allow Him permission to draw us out from anywhere. In fact, Jeremiah 31:3 tells us that in His *everlasting love* for us, *He draws us* **to Himself** *with lovingkindness*. The [MSG] even says that while we're out *looking for a place to rest*, we find that **God is actually looking for us**! We see this in other examples within Scripture also.

In the story of the prodigal's son in Luke 15:20, the father sees his son returning home after foolishly squandering his inheritance, and *while he is still a long way off*, the father *runs to embrace him and kiss him*, restoring him in spite of his mistakes to a sonship status within his household. In order to see him from so far off, that father, like our Father God with His loving plans for us, was watching and waiting in expectation to see him return so that he could help him and restore him. First John 3:1 [AMP] says *see what an incredible quality of love the Father has given, shown, and bestowed upon us that we should be counted as the children of God, and so we are!*

Matthew 18:12-14 and Luke 15:4-7 tell us about a shepherd who has one hundred sheep. He realizes one of his sheep is lost. Even though he still has ninety-nine sheep remaining, he relentlessly *goes to look for his one lost sheep until he finds it, and when he has found it, he joyfully lays it across his shoulders to carry it home, bringing all of his friends together to celebrate*. In John 10:14-16, Jesus tells us emphatically that He is *the Good Shepherd Who knows and recognizes His sheep and is known and recognized by them*. He says that He *gathers us and brings us unto Him as we listen to His voice and pay attention to His call*.

In Matthew 13:44, Jesus tells a parable about *the kingdom of Heaven*, comparing it to *a very precious treasure hidden in a field, which a man found and hid again, and in his ecstatic joy, he goes and sells all that he has to buy that field and secure that treasure for himself*. Certainly, in this we can see that we should go all in for the things of God as if we are securing that treasure for ourselves, but in reciprocity, **this is what Jesus has done for us**. He left His status and position in Heaven to 'buy the whole field' to obtain and secure YOU and ME as His everlasting treasure. *For the joy set before Him—us—He endured the cross* (Hebrews 12:2).

It doesn't matter how far away we think we've strayed or how deeply we feel life has buried us, Jesus is so near, so ready, so **eager** from the **very innermost core of His being** to bridge any gap in an instant, to rescue us, to restore us, to heal us, to **prove** His love for us. And Father God, *Who did not withhold or spare even His own Son but gave Him up for us all, will He not also with Him freely and graciously give us all things* (Romans 8:32)?

So, we are **never** too far away from God. He has gone to great and incomprehensible lengths to make the distance between us short so that He can immediately reach us. We have not made too many mistakes to start over. The reset button is waiting, invitingly, for us to press it today.

Lie: I just can't do this anymore.

Truth: I have felt this way more times than I can count—after I was brutally attacked, when my marriage fell apart, when my child was struggling, when people who were supposed to care about me were spreading untrue and hurtful rumors, when struggles seemed to last indefinitely and I couldn't see an ending point for them, when my own mistakes caused me extreme pain. In these critical junctures—these times of deep stress—the temptation to quit, to give up, or to even wonder if maybe dying would be easier than living was very tangible and almost overwhelming.

In times like these, we wobble between trying to ignore our feelings and trudge on or over-indulging in them to the point that they become all we can see. Somewhere between the "suck it up, buttercup!" thinking and the excessive 'need' to validate and work through each of our feelings are the answers and balance we're sometimes lacking. Neither approach in their extremes is helpful.

If we don't acknowledge the feelings, we can't proactively handle them, and we are in essence not acknowledging our self-worth—we're saying we're not important enough to matter. But if we try to hang on to them too tightly, it can lead to immense grief and self-pity which can be paralyzing and smothering. The devil will throw a pity party that can last indefinitely and cost way more than we can afford (in time, in missed opportunities, in greater loss than we are already grieving) if we choose to attend. Prolonged stress can wreak all sorts of havoc in so many areas of our lives.

If I'm honest with myself, in the times when I didn't have the strength or energy to take another step and felt completely hopeless, I was feeling alone and thinking I needed to be able to get through everything **by myself**. This type of anxiety can be very isolating. I was attending that huge pity party and listening to the 'woe is me' narrative that satan whispers to us in first person to see if we'll accept it as our own inner voice instead of his manipulative masquerade.

Everyone struggles at one time or another. Everyone has good days and bad days, triumphs and tragedies. Sometimes life is painful. Being a Christian doesn't exempt us from that, but through Christ it does give us a stability to endure and transcend our problems (Colossians 2:5 [AMP]), a peace which passes understanding (Philippians 4:7), and ammunition to be both proactive and reactive as we learn to magnify God above the magnitude of our problems (Psalm 34:3).

In addition, as Christians we have the wisdom and the supernatural power of the Creator of the universe, both of which would not otherwise be available to us apart from God. Need a Red Sea parted (Exodus 14:21-22)? Need time to stand still for your victory (Joshua 10:13)? Need a giant defeated in your life (1 Samuel 17:50)? Need the building plans for an ark that can preserve a remnant of creation and carry your family safely through a flood (Genesis 6-8)? The truth is that we don't have to get through **anything** alone. God is powerful enough to help us with everything we need!

We can't let suicidal feelings isolate us. First Corinthians 10:13 [NLT] ensures us that the things we face in our lives *are no different from what others experience*, that *God is faithful to not allow it to be more than we can stand*, and that *He will show us a way out*—His way out—*so that we can endure*. God will help us through everything we face and give us the wisdom we need when we ask Him (James 1:5). Just like He got Shadrach, Meshach, and Abednego out of the fiery furnace unharmed (Daniel 3:16-28). And Daniel safely out of the lion's den (Daniel 6:16-23). And a whole host of other biblical examples who trusted Him faithfully through the situations they encountered (Hebrews 11).

And me out of every single thing I've ever faced no matter how overwhelming it seemed at first. Sometimes His help was miraculous and instant; other times, it was practical and ordinary and seemed slow in coming. But I've never regretted trusting Him within all of my circumstances.

I've learned to trust His timing as well. Have you ever noticed how fickle time can be? I can stick something into the microwave to reheat for a minute or two and it seems like an eternity while I'm standing there waiting for it. I can have two minutes left before I need to walk out the door to get somewhere on time, and it seems literally like two seconds have passed. Learning to wait (and wait well) is a necessary life skill.

Isaiah 42:3 promises that *a bruised reed He will not break, and a dimly burning wick He will not quench; He will faithfully bring forth justice in Truth.* I've felt so bruised at times, like my wick was dimly burning and in danger of going out. What a comfort to know that He notices and promises to help! The ^{MSG} says *He won't brush aside the bruised and the hurt, and He won't disregard the small or insignificant, but He'll steadily and firmly set things right. He won't tire out and He won't quit.* If God is not quitting, we can't quit either! We have to give Him time to steady us, to bring us to better places and happier times.

From a practical and helpful standpoint, we just have to live day by day, twenty-four hours at a time. Jesus Himself encourages us to *not worry or be overly concerned about tomorrow because it will take care of itself*, and *God will help us deal with whatever hard things come up when the time comes* (Matthew 6:34 $^{KJV, MSG}$). We can do anything for twenty-four hours, especially when Philippians 4:13 ^{AMPC} promises us that we have *strength for all things through Christ Who strengthens and empowers us, making us ready for and equal to anything through Him Who infuses inner strength into us*.

The ways in which God empowers us include not only His strength, but also His grace, mercy, favor, love, wisdom, and forgiveness. And the *fruits of the Spirit* (*love, joy, peace, patience, kindness, goodness, faithfulness, gentleness, and self-control*) are available to us in abundant measure (Galatians 5:22-23). All of these things come in never-ending supply if we stay plugged in to Him (John 15:5-6). *They are new every morning* (Lamentations 3:23)!

Jesus tells us in John 6:35 that He is *the Bread of Life*, that when we come to Him, we *will never be hungry and when we believe in Him, we will never be thirsty for He will sustain us spiritually*. Just like the children of Israel were to gather their bread, their manna, every morning in the wilderness (Exodus 16:11-21), we can ask God for our daily bread (our daily wisdom, grace, mercy, and direction) (Matthew 6:11). He will be faithful to help us through these twenty-four hours and the next, and the next, and the next. Daily, He will give us grace and wisdom to do what we need to do—our part—while He does the things only He can do—His part. **And things will get better!** *He always causes us to triumph* (2 Corinthians 2:14).

Then, inside each new day, we'll see a breathtaking sunset, or hear a child's laughter, or have other heart-warming moments that we'll be glad we hung around for. We **can** do this! **You** can do this! Life is a gift meant to be treasured and lived, and we can do all things through Him.

Lie: Everyone would be better off without me.

Truth: Suicide is not really a solution. It causes many more problems than it could ever solve. It permanently ends the life of the person who chooses it, and it forever negatively impacts everyone connected to him or her with immense grief, regret, sorrow, and abandonment. It leaves a gaping hole filled with confusion and pain as family members and friends wonder how they could have helped, what they could have noticed or done differently, and how they could have prevented the death of their loved one. They feel like they've failed this person and that this person has failed them. It leaves behind it a wake of immense negativity, anger, and pain.

This is no way to leave our family or friends.

I have often felt like everyone would be better off without me, or the world would be a better place if I hadn't been born, since my parents were young and careless, and my conception wasn't planned.

But it is simply, plainly, a **lie from the pit of hell**.

As we read before, **God planned us** *before the foundations of the world* (Ephesians 1:4). **He has always loved us and intended for us to be here, now.** In Ephesians 2:10 ^{AMP}, we see that *we are His workmanship—His own master work, a work of art—created in Christ Jesus for good works,* *which God planned and prepared for us ahead of time so we can take the paths He has set out and walk in them, living a good life which He has prearranged and made ready for us to live.*

Each of us is God's masterpiece, and each of us has good things planned for us that make us vitally important to God and others. The world needs me, and the world needs you. I repeat, the world needs you! Say that out loud to yourself: *The world needs me! I am important and valuable, and God created me for such a time as this*! Just like Esther was created for the time in which she lived (Esther 4:14), we are created for our time. Just as Jesus was conceived when the fullness of time came for Him to be born (Galatians 4:4), you were born in the fullness of time within God's plan for your life. God predetermined you before He created this earth, and at just the right time, you came. It's not chance. It's not a mistake. God planned us eons ago.

And whether we are world-changers in the broad sense of the word, or whether we change a more limited scope of the world around us, there are people who need us, love us, and live better lives because we are here. Like the saying, "To the world you may be one person, but to one person, you are the world." Or as Mother Theresa said, "Not all of us can do great things, but we can all do small things with great love."

We all affect one another, and we all have the chance to make life beautiful together. One of my favorite movies is *It's a Wonderful Life* with Jimmy Stewart and Donna Reed. It paints such a deep truth into its story line of how we all impact one another without even realizing it. When the main character decides suicide is his best choice, an angel steps in to intervene at just the right time. He then decides it would be better if he'd never been born. The angel promptly grants his wish, and he sees firsthand how different and empty the lives of everyone he loves would have been without him. It's then that he realizes just how lucky and blessed he and everyone in his life truly are because of the interactions they've had together and the ways they've impacted one another.

If we really have been a burden to those around us, we can work to fix it. If we have made choices that hurt those we love, we can work to make better choices with God's help. Allowing the Truth and transforming power within God's Word to renew our minds (Romans 12:2), straighten out our thinking, and guide our actions and choices will make everything better. Minute by minute, day by day, choice by choice.

And when we mess up, we can start again. Philippians 1:6 assures us *we can be confident and certain that God, Who began this good work within us, will continue to perfect and complete it until it is finally finished.* That's a solution that really solves issues. That's a plan that truly works for everyone's benefit. We are all better and stronger together!

Lie: I've been too unfaithful to God for Him to forgive me.

Truth: Whether we've been willfully wrong or we've just royally messed up, God is always faithful! In 2 Timothy 2:13, we see that *even if we are unfaithful, He remains faithful, for He cannot deny Who He is*— faithfulness is such a part of His character that He is always full of faith and never wavers in His desire to be faithful to us.

The caution is that if we turn our backs on Him, we may very well be tying His hands to help us. Remember that *the Word is a two-edged sword* (Hebrews 4:12), and on one side is blessing but the other side is curse (Deuteronomy 28). God's Word is like a line drawn right down the middle of existence. It sets a standard and always brings justice. Impartially, it is either working for us or against us, and our choices are the deciding factor. Galatians 6:7 ^{NIV, MSG} explains that *a man reaps what he sows—what a person plants, he will harvest. Whoever sows to the flesh will **from the flesh** reap destruction; whoever sows to the Spirit will reap **real life**, eternal life. The mind governed by the flesh is death, but the mind governed by the Spirit is life and peace* (Romans 8:6 ^{NIV}).

*Today I have given you the choice between life and death, between blessings and curses. Now I call on Heaven and earth to witness the choice you make. Oh, that you would **choose life**, so that you and your descendants might live* (Deuteronomy 30:19 NLT)! God wants us to daily choose life and blessing because He knows the elusive subtlety and temptation which sin presents when we are not diligent against it. It works to drive a wedge into our relationship with Him.

We don't want to give sin the chance to harden our hearts or satan the opportunity to condemn us out of being able to accept God's willingness and desire to make things right for us. This is what happened to both Esau (Hebrews 12:17) and Judas (Matthew 27:3-5) in their situations. Condemnation is one of satan's most powerful lies to try to hinder us and keep us from accepting God's mercy.

If our hearts condemn us, telling us we can't be forgiven, *God is greater than our hearts, and knows all things* (1 John 3:20 NKJV). *Whenever our hearts make us feel guilty, and remind us of our failures, we know that God is much greater and more merciful than our conscience, and He knows everything there is to know about us* (TPT). He understands us!

Thankfully, when we mess up, *we have an Advocate with the Father, Jesus Himself, Who will intercede for us* (1 John 2:1). *When He served as a sacrifice for our sins, He solved the sin problem for good—not only ours, but the whole world's* (MSG). Romans 5:8 AMP tells us that *God clearly shows and proves His own love for us by the fact that while we were sinners, Christ died for us.*

Because of this, if *we freely admit our sins when His light uncovers them, He will be faithful to forgive us **every time** and cleanse us from all unrighteousness* (1 John 1:9 TPT). So then, we can *come boldly unto the throne of grace, that we may obtain mercy, and find grace to help in time of need* (Hebrews 4:16 KJV).

Now that we know what we have—Jesus, this great High Priest with ready access to God—let's not let it slip through our fingers. We don't have a priest who is out of touch with our reality. He's been through weakness and testing, experienced it all—all but the sin. So let's walk right up to Him and get what He is so ready to give. Take the mercy, accept the help (Hebrews 4:16 ᴹˢᴳ). Find within Him our place of repentance, acceptance, and restoration. I've heard it said that the only sins we can't be forgiven of are the sins we won't repent of. He's already given Himself to redeem us and paid for the sins of the entire world.

Therefore, know without any doubt and understand that the Lord your God, He is God, the faithful God, and He keeps His covenant and His steadfast lovingkindness to a thousand generations with those who love Him and keep His commandments (Deuteronomy 7:9 ᴬᴹᴾ).

His tender compassions never fail, and His faithfulness is beyond measure, so that we may say that He is our portion and our inheritance, good to those who wait confidently for Him, and seek Him on the authority of God's Word (Lamentations 3:22-25 ᴬᴹᴾ).

We see that Jesus has already solved our sin issues so that we can be forgiven and free from them, without condemnation, to *go and sin no more* (John 8:11). Even when we mess up, sin will not keep us from the faithfulness of God if we turn to Him on the authority of His Word because His faithfulness lasts for a thousand generations. That's not running out any time soon.

Lie: I've got to get my life right, and then I can give it to God.

Truth: That's completely backward, putting the cart before the horse. It is a misperception to think that we have to try to fix ourselves or clean ourselves up before we can present ourselves to God, or that we even **can** on our own. It comes from the whispering voice of condemnation that satan speaks to us and from the shame we often feel when things are a mess.

The fear is that God may reject us otherwise. If we are too big of a mess, will He want us? Resoundingly—emphatically, yes, He will! He does! Our condition is not a surprise to Him. He knows everything about us, and He wants and loves us anyway. Remember that He's loved us since *before the foundation of the world* (Ephesians 1:4). While we were still unaware of Him, *still powerless to help ourselves*, Father God sent Jesus to rescue us (Romans 5:6, Ephesians 2:5).

He didn't, and doesn't, wait for us to get ready. He presented Himself when we were far too weak and rebellious to do anything to get ourselves ready. And even if we hadn't been so weak, we wouldn't have known what to do anyway (Romans 5:6 MSG). *You see, at just the right time, Christ died for the ungodly* (NIV).

In truth, we need God's grace to help us change. Remember that His grace is a supernatural empowering that helps us accomplish what we need to accomplish. He puts His super on top of our natural so that we have His supernatural assistance and support. *It is by His grace through our faith that we are saved; not of ourselves, it is the gift of God* (Ephesians 2:8). He knows we can't do it on our own, and He lovingly, wisely, doesn't expect us to.

He begins the good work within us and then is faithful to complete it (Philippians 1:6). His Word is *transforming*; it makes the changes within us (Romans 12:2). It *washes* us (Ephesians 5:26). Jesus goes *before us to make the crooked places straight and the rough places smooth* (Isaiah 40:4, 45:2) so we should not attempt to fix ourselves before we receive His help. *He anoints our head with oil* (Psalm 23:5), and the anointing *removes burdens and destroys yokes of bondage* (Isaiah 10:27). Jesus is anointed to help us, to heal us, to deliver us, and to work with us to make a message out of our messes, a testimony out of our tests (Isaiah 61:1, Luke 4:18).

He bids us to *come unto Him* **while** *we are weary and heavy-burdened so that we can take His gentle yoke* of liberty and *rest upon us* (Matthew

11:28-29) and work **with** Him to make our lives better. *Walk with Me and work with Me—watch how I do it. Learn the unforced rhythms of grace* (MSG). We don't have to make ourselves presentable apart from Him or before we come to Him in order to access His help. The finished work of Christ is enough for every need we will ever have!

Lie: God is keeping a record of my sins, and they are too many and too large to overcome.

Truth: The wages of sin is death, but Jesus, thankfully, paid those wages for us! There isn't a sin too large for His sacrifice to cover, and He has paid for all of the sins of the world. Yours—no matter how many they may number—are included within His offering. In 1 Peter 2:24 AMP, we see that *He personally carried our sins in His body on the cross, willingly offering Himself on it as a sacrifice so that we might die to sin and become immune from its penalty and power and live for righteousness. He used His servant body to carry our sins to the Cross so we could be rid of sin and free to live the right way* (MSG).

When we ask Him to forgive us, He erases any sin that was on our record, leaving us *white as snow* (Isaiah 1:18). In Psalm 103:10, 12 AMP, we see that *He does not deal with us according to our sins as we* would otherwise *deserve, nor place their punishment upon us. As far as the east is from the west, so far has He removed our transgressions from us.* That's *farther than a sunrise to a sunset* (TPT)!

In Isaiah 43:25 NLT, God says, *"I—yes, I alone—will blot out your sins for My own sake and will never think of them again."* *"I don't keep a list of your sins* (MSG)*."*

Micah 7:19 MSG promises that God *wipes our slate clean of guilt because mercy is His specialty—what He loves most. He stamps out our wrongdoing and sinks our sins to the bottom of the ocean.*

All that is required of us is to come to Him and accept the forgiveness He so willingly wants to give us. That's our part. The rest—His part—He's already done! If you've prayed the prayer within the pages of this book, you can be assured that your sins are already forgiven. If you haven't, then pray now. Romans 10:9 promises that *if you will confess with your mouth Jesus as Lord and believe in your heart that God raised Him from the dead, you will be saved*.

> Dear Heavenly Father, Lord Jesus, and Holy Spirit, please forgive me of my sins. I call upon You for salvation, and I confess Jesus as my Lord, believing that God raised Him from the dead. I also ask You to fill me with Your Holy Spirit to be my Guide and Teacher! In Jesus' Name, Amen!

Psalm 32:2 ᴹˢᴳ assures us that we *can count ourselves lucky because God holds nothing against us when we hold nothing back from Him*. There is no amount of sin that can separate us from His unfailing love.

Lie: I am a victim.

Truth: Though many of us have been victimized by circumstances and people, Christ doesn't leave us in that broken condition. He doesn't want us to have a victim-mentality, but rather a victor-mentality. He offers us healing and redemption. God is a god of restoration and victory. Psalm 103:13 ᴹˢᴳ promises that *God makes everything come out right; He puts victims back on their feet*. Second Corinthians 2:14 promises that God will *always cause us to triumph* when we place our faith and trust in Him, leading us *in one perpetual victory parade* ⁽ᴹˢᴳ⁾. After listing many disadvantages (peril, tribulation, distress, etc.), Romans 8:37 promises that in *all of these things we are more than conquerors* and that *overwhelming, surpassing victory is ours through Him Who loved us enough to die for us. If God be for us* (and He is!), *who can be against us* (verse 31)? Christ will take us from being a vic~~tim~~ to a VIC**TOR** as we allow Him.

Lie: I just can't 'see' how things can get any better, how my life can improve.

Truth: Sometimes when we can't see, it is because *the god of this world, satan, is working* overtime *to blind us* (2 Corinthians 4:4). He wants us to think it is foolishness to believe in things we can't see (1 Corinthians 1:18), to be afraid to believe, or to feel too overwhelmed or distracted to consider believing. But, thankfully, just as He did in Genesis when He said *let there be light* (Genesis 1:3), God is still commanding *light to come forth in our darkness* (2 Corinthians 4:6).

God is master at giving sight to our blindness. He promises to open *the eyes of our heart so that we can see the hope of His calling* (Ephesians 1:18) and to *flood our hearts with light so that we can understand the confident hope that He gives us* (NLT). Romans 8:15 NIV assures us that He is a *God of hope* and He will *fill us with all joy and peace* **as we trust in Him** so that *we can overflow with hope by the power of the Holy Spirit*.

He can *open doors that no man can shut* (Isaiah 22:22, Revelation 3:8). He came *to give us abundant life, to the full, until it overflows* (John 10:10 AMP). *He is able to do exceedingly, abundantly above all that we can ask, think, or imagine when we allow His power to work within us* (Ephesians 3:20 AMP).

He will *make a way* where there seems to be no way—*a way through the sea, a path through the mighty waters* (Isaiah 43:16), *a road in the wilderness, and rivers in the desert* (verse 19). It doesn't matter what circumstances we're coming from or the condition of our hearts. He promises to help us forget the past and bring us into new places in Him (verses 18-19).

We can ask God to show us, just as the psalmist did in Psalm 25:4-5 when he requested *show me Your ways, O Lord; teach me Your paths. Guide me in Your Truth and teach me, for You are the God of my salvation.* The ᵀᴾᵀ reads *Lord, direct me throughout my journey so I can experience Your plans for my life. Reveal the life-paths that are pleasing to You. Escort me along the way; take me by the hand and teach me. For You are the God of my increasing salvation; I have wrapped my heart into Yours!*

God wants to show us His love and give us hope in Him so that our *hope can be an anchor for our souls—an unbreakable spiritual lifeline* (Hebrews 6:19 ᴷᴶⱽ, ᴹˢᴳ)—as He brings us forward into the blessings and good plans He's always had for us (Jeremiah 29:11) and works to make things new and better for us (Isaiah 43:19).

And now to Him Who can keep you on your feet, standing tall in His bright presence, fresh and celebrating—to our one God, our only Saviour, through Jesus Christ, our Master, be glory, majesty, strength, and rule before all time, and now, and to the end of all time. Yes. (Jude 1:24 ᴹˢᴳ)

♥

Notes:

Notes: